Nantucket Looms

Nantucket Looms

A Legacy of Style

With
LINDA JANE HOLDEN

Foreword by
MITCHELL OWENS

Principal Photography by
MATT KISIDAY

RIZZOLI
NEW YORK

New York · Paris · London · Milan

We dedicate this book
to Liz, Bill, and Andy,
for sharing their
special world with us
so that we may share
it with others.

Contents

Foreword

by

MITCHELL OWENS

Somewhere in my disorganized files is a scrap of handwoven linen, not much larger than the palm of my hand. Slightly nubby, somewhat reminiscent of slubbed silk, it is the shifting color of sun-bleached sand—not quite beige, not quite white—yet it is anything but neutral, either in tone or in texture. It has presence and depth and character, silently coaxing me to examine it more closely, to understand what are, to me, the mysteries of the weaver's art. Despite its small size, that scrap carries unlikely worlds within its crisscrossing threads, linking the Staatliches Bauhaus in Germany, that early twentieth-century turning point for modernist aesthetics, to Nantucket Looms, a bustling little shop that has anchored a block of a Massachusetts town's cobblestoned Main Street for more than a half century.

From covetable whisper-quiet fabrics to the head-turning interior design projects that emphasize understated elegance, Nantucket Looms exhibits a passion for meticulous craftmanship that has never wavered since the firm was brought into being in 1968 by Bill Euler and Andy Oates, an island couple with an appreciation for the artisanal that bordered on religious fervor. Indeed, Oates had studied weaving in the 1940s at North Carolina's illustriously arty yet woefully short-lived Black Mountain College. One of his instructors was Bauhaus alumna Anni Albers, that high priestess of textile art, who once said of her own works, "I try to make them as anonymous as possible."

Filtered through Oates, passed on to his associates Sam Kasten and Rebecca Jusko Peraner, and disseminated to a new generation of studio weavers,

Albers's philosophy of blending quality with discretion infuses every product made by Nantucket Looms and every room it decorates. Some of the firm's most representative fabrics for the home ("from the airiest of mohairs to the sturdiest of tweeds," a newspaper article once observed) have been rapturously subtle and justly celebrated for their handwrought modesty. That being said, they are equally powerful in their unadorned honesty, their magical textures, their felicitous marriages of warp and weft, and their loyal embrace of beauty that whispers rather than shouts. Small wonder that leading American tastemakers such as Bunny Mellon, Jacqueline Kennedy Onassis, and Billy Baldwin—the idolized interior decorator who counted both women among his clients—were fervent Nantucket Looms disciples, and why so many of today's designers and architects count themselves equally smitten. As Oates once said of his studio's hallmark line, "It appeals to a special kind of craftsman the way it appeals to a special kind of person."

Billy Baldwin's former business partner, Arthur H. Smith, gave me the Nantucket Looms handwoven linen and ramie ribbed fabric scrap decades ago, telling me that it was one of the master's favorite materials, bearing witness to a dedication to stylish simplicity that he and his mentor shared. Since then, I've crossed paths with many designers who not only catch their breath at the mention of Nantucket Looms and its rich history but, like me, can recount the very first time they were introduced to the chicly modest, quietly sensational fabrics that are still woven by hand on a storied speck of rock and sand off the coast of Massachusetts.

NANTUCKET LOOMS

NANTUCKET ISLAND, MASSACHUSETTS 02554

16 MAIN STREET TELEPHONE 617 228-1908

Name: S 1c

PAGE 15: Archival fabrics from the early years at Nantucket Looms. Andy Oates's white linen and ramie ribbed fabric samples are featured in hues of navy, ecru, and soft ivory in silk or jute fibers. Several variations of this type of simple weave are still handwoven at the studio today. **ABOVE:** The colors of the variegated cashmere throw—from dark blues and greens to light grays—give it a lustrous shimmering look like a marlin. The throw adds a layer of comfort to this classic coastal-style living room. Seasonal fresh-cut flowers, a book, a magnifying glass, and a garland of wooden beads dress up the coffee table. **OPPOSITE:** A shingled porch wall is used as the backdrop to display an assortment of mohair throws woven in the signature colors of Nantucket—fog gray, ivory, sage, and sky blue. Mohair, which is a luxury fiber prized for its lustrous sheen, comes from the hair of the angora goat. It is warm in winter and cool in summer.

1

A Nantucket Style is Born

ARTISTRY
AND
CRAFTSMANSHIP
EMBRACED

There's an old saying on Nantucket that lightning only strikes once. And one of those times was in the 1960s when an American style was born. It was an understated aesthetic, one that harmonized with the timeless appeal of quality American arts and classic craftsmanship, a curated look of bespoke and discovered objects that reflected the personality of the collector and the rich history of the island. This appealing genre of style emerged amid the formality of the Georgian, Federal, and Greek Revival architecture of the historic downtown. Influencers such as Bunny Mellon, Hubert de Givenchy, Princess Grace of Monaco, Billy Baldwin, and even former First Ladies, including Jacqueline "Jackie" Kennedy Onassis, Claudia Alta "Lady Bird" Johnson, and Hillary Rodham Clinton, were drawn to the whimsical mix of pared-down homespun craftsmanship, the perfect complement to the island's nostalgic maritime history.

This distinctive style was the brainchild of master weaver Andrew Oates and businessman William Euler, owners of Nantucket Looms, a retail shop that featured Nantucket-related objects for the home as well as a production weaving studio where Andy taught residents the fine art of weaving and where one-of-a-kind handwoven textiles were produced. Showcasing the work of local artists and artisans was at the heart of Andy and Bill's vision for Nantucket Looms—and for decorating their own homes. Their look was merely a reflection of their lifestyle, a life well lived on an island by the sea and one with a high regard and appreciation for simplicity, natural beauty, and sense of place. They prized minimalism and refinement, along with high quality in every aspect

of their lives. They didn't reside at expensive addresses or drive fancy cars, but they lived with beautiful products such as leather goods, quality drinking glasses, and luxurious linens, creating a lovely way of life and a stylishness that transcends time. As Andy and Bill's distinctive look caught on, it became known as Nantucket cottage style, a term that evolved over time.

Bill and Andy owned two houses on Nantucket: No. 3 Bear Street and The Shack. Bear Street, formally known as the Tristram Bunker House, is one of the older houses on the island; a lean-to style structure originally built at Capaum Harbor in 1720 and later moved to its present site on the edge of town in 1756. On the first floor there is a primitive oversized fireplace where the cooking was once done, herbs were hung to dry, wood was stored, and cold hands and feet could be warmed by a kindled fire. Other special features include original wood paneling, millwork, wide-plank flooring, and a root cellar. And memories. Lots of memories for many lucky people. The Bear Street house had a cozy ambiance and was a warm and welcoming setting for Nantucket Looms annual Christmas parties and frequent get-togethers of friends, neighbors, and family.

Bill and Andy's summertime retreat was a beachside cottage they called The Shack. It was a place where friends were invited to spend lazy days in the sun, swimming, and enjoying simple, fresh meals often prepared by Andy, who was a great cook.

Today's Nantucket Looms Chief Executive Officer Bess Clarke was quite young when she and her mom, Elizabeth "Liz" Winship, then the Nantucket Looms shop manager, visited with Andy and Bill at The Shack on Sunday afternoons. "Being invited to The Shack was a real privilege and was my mom's favorite place," Bess

PAGES 18–19: A path winds through the uneven terrain of the grass-covered moors to reach 40th Pole Beach. **PREVIOUS PAGES:** The Nantucket Looms weaving studio at 16 Main Street, seen in the mid-1960s when the operation was owned by the Cloth Company. Andy Oates, who later became a co-owner of Nantucket Looms, is seated at the Macomber loom in the foreground. **ABOVE:** Andy looks up from weaving an overshot pattern. The pattern name describes a weaving process of shooting several weft yarns over the warp yarns all at once, resulting in a geometric design, a process commonly used in the mid-1700s to create coverlets. **LEFT:** Bill Euler was known for his warm personality and savvy business sense. His vision for a sustainable year-round business supporting local artists continues today.

said. "We would go out to The Shack around happy hour to visit with Bill and Andy and watch the setting of the sun over the ocean. Bill drank martinis or vodka with Clamato juice, and they always served very simple but elegant food such as beautiful cheese boards, good crackers, and tasty olives." She added, "They didn't have a lot of things, but they enjoyed the best of everything."

A former bathhouse built in the late 1800s, the structure was moved to Madequecham Valley Road, where there is a remarkable view of the South Shore. Primitive, yet elegant, it was a relaxing place for peaceful souls, where time was measured by moments and where the ambiance of Andy and Bill's Nantucket cottage style emerged. Their chosen palette of colors reflected the charm, moods, and aura of the island: the blue shades of sea and sky, and the gray tones of the fog, weathered house shingles, and whales swimming nearby offshore.

ABOVE: The golden hour descends on the cottage, called The Shack, owned by Andy and Bill, Nantucket Looms partners. The home was originally a bathhouse that had been moved to Madequecham Valley Road on the southern shore of the island. Andy, who was an accomplished photographer, took this image.

The range of colors that inspired them came from the bricks and cobblestones, sand and shells, the cranberries of autumn, the roses of summertime, Queen Anne's lace, hollyhocks, and hydrangea blossoms. Amid weathered wooden tables, natural fiber rugs, and the accoutrements of their island style, Andy and Bill curated their collections of shorebird carvings, seashells, marbles, and feathers, along with locally produced crafts, artwork, and textiles.

Nantucket Looms Chief Creative Officer and Principal Designer Stephanie Hall described Andy and Bill's, and what later became Liz's, cottage look as "a unique combination of simplicity and elegance where the design objective was to avoid anything that was over-the-top ornate and to have a few key pieces that were, in their own basic nature, inherently beautiful." Being at The Shack inspired Stephanie's own iteration of cottage style, which can now be seen in the homes that she and the Nantucket Looms interiors team design today.

When former First Lady Jacqueline Kennedy Onassis visited the shop at 16 Main Street, she often ventured up the stairs to the second-floor studio where the magic was happening—where the weavers were working and where there was an abundance of merchandise that wasn't yet on

OPPOSITE: An American decorative punched-design tole lantern that hangs from painted rafters adds interest to the monochromatic passage leading to the back sitting room at The Shack. Andy's framed photographs of architectural elements are displayed on a wall covered with painted wood planks. **ABOVE:** A grouping of handwoven lightship baskets, an important element of Andy and Bill's cottage style, were once purposeful but are now coveted for their ornamental and historic charm. The painting by Leigh Palmer is now owned by Nantucket Looms partner Stephanie Hall. Kenneth Layman's landscape is displayed on the rocking chair.

LEFT: Part of an exquisite collection of miniature baskets, some of them nesting, feature scrimshaw that is sentimental to the collector. A combination of antique ivory and fossilized mammoth bone is used on some of the lids, handles, rims, and bases.

ABOVE: Nantucket Looms was originally located at 16 Main Street on the corner of Washington Street, known as Gardiner's Corner. The compass rose billboard was attached to the side of the building in 1930 by H. Marshall Gardiner, the owner. It has a connection to Nantucket's whaling past with its way of mapping out distances on the island and showing mileages measured by land and sea miles to ports of call around the globe. **LEFT:** A view of a special planter, originally a fountain, in front of 16 Main Street in the 1970s. Donated anonymously to the town in 1885, it has stood in several locations. The planter, made of iron, has a unique design. There is a large basin for horses to drink from and a lower one for dogs. Cups were attached with a chain for people to drink out of.

ABOVE: Using the Nantucket Looms business model, Leslie Tillett and his wife, D.D. Tillett, were the designers and owners of House of T Fabrics in Manhattan and worked with Jacqueline "Jackie" Kennedy Onassis to establish Design Works with the Bedford Stuyvesant Restoration Corporation in 1969. Tillett is shown giving a lecture at Design Works to attendees that include Daphne Shepard, Barbara "Babe" Paley (in striped dress), and Betsey Whitney in the front row, Diana Vreeland, editor-in-chief of *Vogue*, Jackie, and Nan Kempner (in back by the window).
RIGHT: Liz Winship with then First Lady Hillary Rodham Clinton during her visit to the shop in 1999.

display. Here, surrounded by the weavers with soothing rhythmic sounds of the floor looms at work, plus the spindles of colorful yarns and the collections of handwoven scarves and throws draped over the stair railing, Jackie was in her element. "She would pull a chair over and stand up on it to see what treasures were hidden on the top shelves and pull things out," former Nantucket Looms weaver Sam Kasten remembered. Jackie knew there was always something new to see at the shop.

The whole idea of Nantucket Looms and how it had revived "old almost forgotten techniques of weaving," as she wrote her former social secretary, Letitia "Tish" Baldrige, was clearly on Mrs. Onasssis's mind in 1969 when she replicated the Nantucket Looms business model at Design Works, her nonprofit in Bedford Stuyvesant, New York, where handmade textiles were produced and local artists from the Bed-Stuy community were brought together. With her trademark commitment to public service, Jackie endeavored to engage the

community by offering education, training, and employment in fabric production at Design Works, mirroring what she had seen at Nantucket Looms. Design Works, which operated from 1969 to 1979, was an affiliate of Robert F. Kennedy's Bedford Stuyvesant Restoration Corporation, a community-driven nonprofit tasked with the revitalization of the New York City neighborhood.

When Andy Oates and Bill Euler retired after twenty-five years at the helm, they gifted the business to Bill's longtime protégé, Liz Winship, the matriarch and personality of the business, whom he nicknamed Mother because of her care—she took him to doctor's appointments and looked after him like a mother. Following in the footsteps of generations of savvy Nantucket women, Liz continued the expansion of her business operation and launched the Nantucket Looms Interior Design Studio in 1998 where she spun straw into gold for her clients, curating their personal visions of Nantucket cottage style, while shrewdly enriching the Nantucket

Looms legacy for the next generation of partners to build upon. The company's distinctive globally recognized interiors style—bespoke handwoven textiles, artisanal furnishings, and local art that exudes the island's heritage—is coveted by today's tastemakers. Their homes, meant to be shared with family and friends, are for entertaining and living beautifully.

Today, Nantucket Looms style is curated in both the retail shop as well as in their interior design studio's projects by Stephanie and her team. She said, "Liz mentored me for over twenty years. I shadowed her in the shop, on buying trips, and on design jobs, embracing all her lessons, as well as what I learned from Andy and Bill, to be passed down to the next generation of talented people who work with us, such as our manager, Thayer Hale." Stephanie works with her Nantucket Looms partners Master Weaver Rebecca Jusko Peraner and CEO Bess Clarke, Liz's daughter. They are joined by talented local artists and artisans, as well as their extraordinary team, creative and imaginative men and women who work

LEFT: A view of Nantucket Looms today at 51 Main Street. On the shop windows is the company's 2018 anniversary logo celebrating fifty years of weaving, design, community, and art. **ABOVE:** Liz Winship, who began working at Nantucket Looms as a shop assistant in 1974 and retired in 2015, continues to be a guiding light with the title owner emeritus.

together to make Nantucket Looms—and Nantucket Island—the enchanting place it is today.

The dream of living on an island in a house by the sea still brings many artists and sun seekers to Nantucket, a Neverland sort of place, one that quickly becomes as familiar as a friend. The historic town is a maze of cobblestoned streets lined with old mansions and shops dating back to the glory days when Nantucket ruled the seas. The sounds of ringing church bells, clanging buoys, and blasts of ferry horns fill the breezy air. Oceanfront properties dot the 82 miles of publicly accessible coastline, and approximately half of the island is protected. The island's beauty and architectural gems are best experienced firsthand. On some days the Grey Lady, a thick fog, rolls in from the sea covering the island in mist. And on other days the sky is a thousand shades of blue. "Little Grey Lady of the Sea," an expression that originated in the twentieth century commonly uses the word "grey," the British spelling. Today the preferred American English spelling is "gray." After sunset, heavenly hosts of stars, planets, and constellations cast a glow over the mysterious atmosphere where each season is in possession of its own treasures, its own particular brand of beauty. Whether in sunshine or in shadow, there's always a feast for the eyes, an inspirational beauty that speaks to the soul.

ABOVE: Partners in business, friends in life, the current generation of leaders at Nantucket Looms (from left to right): Master Weaver Rebecca Jusko Peraner, Chief Creative Officer and Principal Designer Stephanie Hall, and Chief Executive Officer Bess Clarke. RIGHT: The elegant yet understated look of Nantucket Looms style is showcased in the retail shop display. Important elements include personal collections, a soft-hued palette, contemporary furnishings, organic textures, handwoven textiles, and local artwork.

LEFT: Easily accessible in the Nantucket Looms Interior Design Studio, a wide assortment of textile samples arranged in varying shades of colors and patterns are a source of inspiration. **FOLLOWING PAGES:** A seasonal centerpiece showcasing Nantucket's favorite flower, the hydrangea, is the focus of this inviting tablescape dressed up with a beautiful set of dinnerware, flatware, wine glasses, and candles in hurricanes for an evening of alfresco dining. Handwoven throws for wrapping up on cool nights are draped over abaca rope dining chairs.

NANTUCKET LORE

In his classic American novel, *Moby Dick*, Herman Melville seemingly rejoiced in his exuberant description of Nantucket when he wrote, "Nantucket! Take out your map and look at it. See what a real corner of the world it occupies; how it stands there, away offshore. . . . Look at it—a mere hillock, an elbow of sand; all beach, without a background." Today Melville's "elbow of sand" is described by scientists as a terminal moraine, which, by definition, is the culmination or remains of a glacier. Melville also wrote about "the wondrous traditional story of how this island was settled" by indigenous people. One story tells about a giant warrior named Maushop, who stretched out along the sandy beaches of Cape Cod one night to sleep. To his dismay, when he awoke in the morning, he discovered that his moccasins had filled with sand during the night and hurled both into the sea. The one that landed nearby became Martha's Vineyard, and the other Nantucket— the Wampanoag word for faraway.

The faraway island was first inhabited by the Wampanoags, an indigenous people. Many of their place names on the island survive today, making it the most concentrated collection of indigenous place names in

this country: Madaket, Quaise, Madequecham, Wauwinet, Miacomet, and Siasconset, to name a few. In 1659 a group of fearless, independent-minded English settlers, seeking economic opportunity and a place where they could govern themselves, purchased a majority of the island from the governor of Martha's Vineyard, while simultaneously negotiating peace treaties with the Wampanoags. Primarily farmers and shepherds by trade, the Proprietors, as the settlers called themselves, settled around Capaum Harbor (today called Capaum Pond) on the North Shore and utilized an ancient practice of casting lots to divide the surrounding landscape into equal parcels or building lots. The remaining land was held in common for farming and grazing sheep.

The scarcity of trees required the English settlers to import wood from New England to construct their two-story houses in lean-to or saltbox styles. These structures were sited with a southern exposure to take advantage of the warmth of the sun and were framed with hand-hewn oak timbers fastened together by mortise-and-tenon joinery. Heavy corner posts of oak supported dark wood ceiling beams that contrasted with the whitewashed interior walls. A centrally located fireplace, used

PAGE 38: A coffee table decorated with a subtle nod to Nantucket's storied past—a book written by Herman Melville. PAGE 39: The welcoming graveled courtyard entrance to the Carriage House, which was originally built as a barn, then converted to a carriage house for horses, and finally turned into a dwelling. The Nantucket Blue shutters remain closed in quieter months but are left open when the homeowners are in residence. LEFT: The 'Sconset Foot Bridge was erected in the 1880s to span Gulley Road and connect the 'Sconset village center with newer houses. The 90-foot bridge, with its sparkling views of the ocean, is a popular tourist attraction today. 'Sconset is the common name for the unincorporated village of Siasconset.

for cooking and for heating, was the heart of the home. It was often from eight to ten feet wide and in the shape of an alcove large enough to hold stores of chopped wood and a bench, making it the warmest place in the house. In the evening after the cooking fire had turned to ash, moonlight flooded down the chimney casting a magical glow across the hearth below. Typically, there were three rooms on the first floor: the parlor, which was a multipurpose room where the family gathered and entertained friends, the keeping room, and kitchen. The rooms would be furnished with spindle back and Windsor chairs, three-legged stools, tables, and canopied beds. Some houses had a grandfather clock, and some had curtains covering the narrow diamond-shaped window openings, or "lights" as they were called. The dirt floors were covered with layers of sand and continuously swept with the swishing hems of the ladies' long skirts. Sometimes fanciful designs were impressed across the sand, giving a painted floor effect. Hook-shaped branches and roots of savin, *juniperus sabina*, were dried and fastened to walls to serve as hooks, or hangers. Additional rooms, including a birthing room and buttery, were often built adjacent to the kitchen at the back of the house and covered with a shed type of roof called a cat slide, which created the lean-to style. Two upstairs chambers, or bedrooms, were reached by climbing a narrow steep set of stairs that wrapped around the centrally located fireplace chimney. A platform mounted on the rooftop, called "a walk," was accessible through a skylight. It provided access to the chimney for extinguishing fires and also served as a lookout to watch for returning ships on the distant horizon.

Textiles were of high value and many families owned spinning wheels and floor looms to weave cloth for their clothing, curtains, and bed and table coverings. Most household objects were of a utilitarian nature, of excellent quality, and made to last. Details that we find quaint today included wooden door latches, rope handrails, wide-plank wood floors, exposed beams, and heavy batten doors with forged iron fittings, critical for protection against the forces of nature.

After one especially fierce storm closed Capaum Harbor in 1720, most of the houses were taken down and then rebuilt a short distance from a new settlement on a larger harbor, which was eventually named Nantucket. Melville recounted this long adhered-to practice in *Moby Dick*, noting "pieces of wood in Nantucket are carried about like bits of the true cross in Rome."

Continued upheavals brought more change to the island. For the settlers, coaxing a livelihood on Nantucket had been a mix of trial and error. Over time the traditional occupations of sheep herding and farming had proven to be unsuccessful. Taking a cue from their friendly neighbors, the Wampanoags, the settlers turned to whaling, a risky and dangerous business. From March to December, numerous pods of whales migrate along the coast of Nantucket, a vast section of ocean that extends to the continental shelf break. What began as a local operation of harvesting beached whales and hunting whales offshore morphed into an international industry in the eighteenth and early nineteenth centuries as this hearty lot of men took to the open seas chasing pods of whales around the globe in search of spermaceti—a superior type of whale oil. Cries of "Thar she blows," and "Nantucket Sleighride," the term used to describe a whaleboat being dragged by a whale, became island vernacular. It was the beginning of the Industrial Age and whale oil, a globally prized source of energy that illuminated cities and lubricated the great machinery of the era, was probably the most lucrative product of the time. This hard-won success transformed a once sleepy harbor into the whaling capital of the world.

At the same time a large part of the whaling community experienced a religious awakening by converting to the Society of Friends, or Quakerism. Mary Coffin Starbuck, a leading figure on the island for decades, had been vehemently opposed to the establishment of any religion to ultimately protect the ability to think independently.

 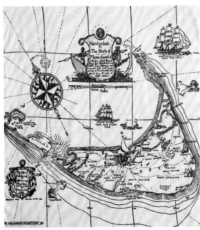 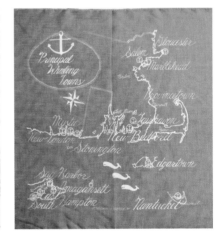

OPPOSITE: A sandy path winds through dunes ending at Brant Point Lighthouse, which sits at the mouth of Nantucket Harbor. At the right is a service building belonging to the US Coast Guard Station at Brant Point. Erected in 1746, the lighthouse is the second oldest in the United States. The sweetly fragrant Rosa Rugosa grows in abundance on the island. ABOVE: In the mid-1960s the Cloth Company and its two affiliated divisions, the Needlery and Nantucket Looms under the Nantucket Historical Trust, produced silk-screened silk scarves in bright colors designed by Leslie Tillett that depicted maps of the area and whaling procedures.

RIGHT: A whimsical collection of items, all made in different periods from antique ivory, that include a domino game piece, pie crimper, sewing needle case, and a game box with dice. The ditty box and a dory are carved out of bone by Mark Sutherland.

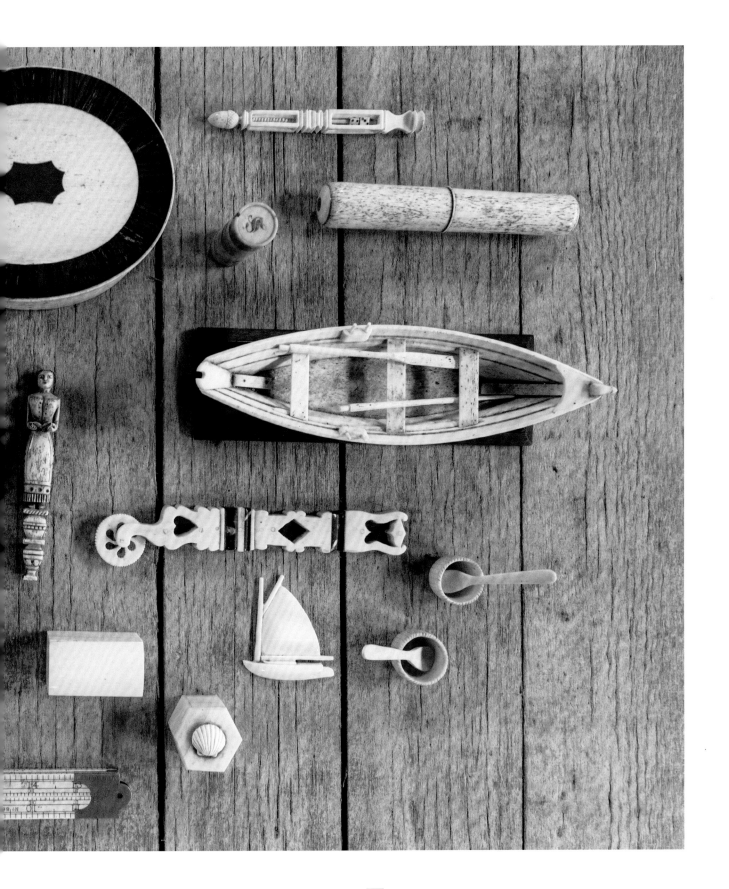

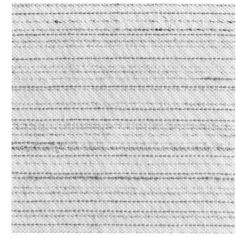

She publicly converted to Quakerism in 1702, wholeheartedly embracing its plain, anti-worldly way of life.

The convergence of the Quaker faith with the astonishing wealth of the whalers had enormous influence on the aesthetic elements of the architecture and design of Nantucket's Colonial era, mirroring the Quaker's simplistic, egalitarian, and austere lifestyle. The decades from 1700 to 1750 were a time of domestic transition as the elements and features of architecture continued to evolve along with the development of Nantucket's downtown. The typical Nantucket house, of which hundreds were built, became distinguished as plain, sturdy asymmetrical structures free of ornamentation. The size of the house was scaled down, built close to the sidewalk or street, and filled the width of the lot. Exterior walls were shingled with a wood board that was left to weather naturally in the salt air to a fine patina of gray. The rear wall was raised to the same height as the front wall and

the steep pitch of the roof was lowered. The front door was placed off-center and topped with a transom window. Windows were typical plank frames and sash, with twelve-over-twelve 6-by-8-inch glass panes. A picket fence capped with a ship's rail enclosed the property.

ABOVE LEFT: The Jared Coffin House (seen here and opposite in 1967), located at the corner of Broad and Centre Streets, was built in 1845 for whaling merchant Jared Coffin and his family. Because his wife preferred not to live there, the family moved to Boston and sold the property. It was then converted into a hotel called the Ocean House. In 1961 the Nantucket Historical Trust bought the property, making it their first restoration project on the island. The trust hired interior designer William Pahlmann and founded Nantucket Looms to produce reproductions of nineteenth-century fabrics from the date of Coffin's occupancy. **ABOVE TOP RIGHT:** This fabric, woven with wool yarn, was used to upholster the wing chairs and other seating. **ABOVE BOTTOM RIGHT:** Some of the coverlets for the guest rooms were woven in a blue overshot pattern out of cotton and wool.

ABOVE: Ulysses Grant, the eighteenth president of the United States, occupied this room at the Ocean House (now called the Jared Coffin House) with his wife, Julia, on their overnight visit to Nantucket in 1874. The redecoration of the Grant Room during the 1960s restoration was inspired by the Nancy McClelland wallpaper, which interior designer William Pahlmann paired with an antique Turkish Oushak rug and a green coverlet handwoven at Nantucket Looms.

At first the decorative arts were merely a practical and utilitarian reflection of this nautical lifestyle, but, as the whaling enterprise prospered, proud hard-working whalers returned home bearing bountiful treasure troves of prized booty from around the globe for their loved ones—hand-carved scrimshaw, shell mosaic art, fabrics, and Chinese porcelains—all of which contributed a worldly and cosmopolitan flair to the interior spaces of their homes.

The whaling industry, the heart of Nantucket's economy, prospered until the mid-1800s when a series of major setbacks began to occur. As the whalers traveled farther, the longer voyages required larger ships to accommodate weightier cargo, resulting in deeper ship drafts, too deep to sail over Nantucket's shallow harbor, forcing the whaleships to unload their cargo in harbors other than Nantucket.

In 1846 what became known as the Great Fire utterly destroyed a third of the town, approximately 250 buildings, and the commercial wharves. Followed by the lure for gold in 1850, the potential to acquire new wealth pulled many Nantucketers West. The discovery of petroleum in Pennsylvania in 1859 eliminated the exigency for whale oil altogether, sending the industry into a steep decline and sounding the death knell almost overnight. The devastation of the American Civil War years from 1860 to 1864 shuttered the island. And then, quietly, as if in a fairy tale, a deep slumber fell over the faraway island, lingering for the next fifty years until the winds of fate blew new life into its once vibrant economy.

The early twentieth-century tourism boom brought a reawakening that lifted Nantucket out of its slump and put it back on the map. The architectural heritage, pristine beaches and natural beauty of the island were rediscovered as grand hotels, supper clubs, quaint developments, and artist colonies sprang up across the island, bringing a new crop of summer visitors and economic opportunity. This renewal sparked an obsession for the glory days of its past as the next generation of Nantucketers discovered a rare time capsule in their midst—over a thousand undisturbed buildings in the Quaker architectural style remained—a lingering shadow of yesteryear.

In 1955 Nantucket became the first town in the state of Massachusetts, and the second town in the United States after Charleston, South Carolina, to establish a historic district governed by legislation, which guaranteed architectural control and protection. At a time when the only year-round jobs available on the island were gathering scallops and working in the building trades, businessman and summer resident Walter Beinecke Jr. established the Nantucket Historical Trust (which no longer exists) to fund the transformation and preservation of Nantucket's downtown and wharves into a thriving tourist economy that would guarantee year-round employment for the islanders. At the core of the plan was a solid commitment to honor the island's historic heritage and natural beauty through architectural projects and conservation programs. The restoration of the downtown area, upper Main Street, and the commercial wharves lit up the island in more ways than one as the Trust took charge through property ownership. Nostalgic Nantucketers fought Beinecke at every turn. Former Nantucket Looms weaver Sam Kasten remembered Beinecke "bought up every straight building that wasn't in a leaning position on the island, and impeccably restored everything—even the wharf," ultimately transforming Nantucket into the world-class resort destination it is today. The undertaking eventually proved to be such a success that President Ronald Reagan awarded the President's Historic Preservation Award in 1988 to Beinecke and the Nantucket Historical Trust in recognition of their efforts to revitalize and preserve Nantucket Island's town center and the wharves.

With its charming coastal vibe and pristine buildings dating from the seventeenth century, the town of Nantucket exudes a rare harmony and dreamy mystique. Everything is on point echoing the glory days of the past when Nantucket was the global whaling capital.

A Fateful Meeting

Nantucket Looms's story began on a wintry evening in 1962 at the Woodbox Inn when Walter Beinecke Jr. and his wife, Mary Ann, invited Andy Oates, the head cook, and Bill Euler, the inn manager, to join them for after-dinner coffee. In a recorded interview about that evening Andy remembered Beinecke asked him, "If you had a lot of money, what would you do on Nantucket?" Andy answered readily, "I know perfectly well what I'd do. I'd start a craft movement." Upon hearing this Mary Ann Beinecke "sat back in her chair and asked, 'Really?'" "Yes," Andy replied, "I'm a weaver." She "dropped her

fork" in surprise because "she was a weaver, too." For Andy, Nantucket was the "perfect place for crafts. With so many people with little to do through long winters, it could be a marvelous spot for weavers and other crafts people." In 1961 the Trust had begun the restoration of

ABOVE: The Woodbox Inn, originally built in 1709 as a one-and-a-half-story saltbox-style house for the George Bunker family, is where the Nantucket Looms story began. As Andy Oates and Bill Euler enjoyed after-dinner coffee at the restaurant there with Mary Ann and Walter Beinecke Jr., who were helping with the restoration of the Jared Coffin House, the idea for a weaving studio, which was eventually called Nantucket Looms, sprang to life. **FOLLOWING PAGES**: This seaside garden located near Pimnys Point, across the harbor from Coatue Point, was designed by Julie Jordin of the Garden Design Company. The stone ha-ha wall is planted with hollyhock, astilbe, and poppies. Beyond the wall towards the harbor are Russian sage, maroon ninebark shrubs, and panicle hydrangea.

the Ocean House hotel, built in 1845 at 29 Broad Street, renaming it for whaling merchant Jared Coffin and transforming it into a state-of-the-art hotel in the Neoclassical style. Under the guidance of Mary Ann Beinecke, the Nantucket Historical Trust set up two schools to teach handweaving and needlework to produce textiles patterned after nineteenth-century fabrics for the Jared Coffin House restoration. Andy managed the weaving school at 16 Main Street which, in 1963, was officially named Nantucket Looms. The Needlery and Nantucket Looms hand-crafted bedspreads, draperies, rugs, and placemats—a total of over 6,000 yards of fabric in two years' time—for the Jared Coffin House restoration.

Andy's idea of creating a marvelous spot for weavers and other craftspeople on Nantucket became the reality it is today. He did, indeed, begin the island's Arts and Crafts movement.

2
Nantucket Looms at Home

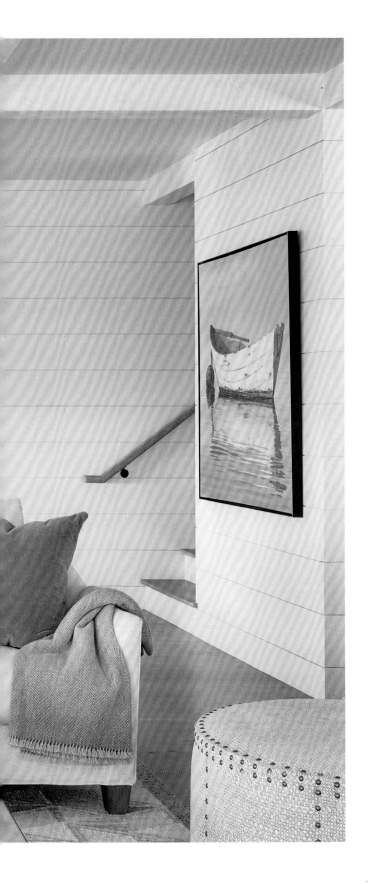

KNUT HOUSE

An Artistic Abode

This two-story house, ca. 1890s, near the harbor bustles with activity in summertime. After a day of sailing, the family enjoys playing games on the four-season porch. Following a complete renovation, aside from the enclosed porch that was lovingly restored to retain its original charm, Knut House, an abbreviation for the family's last name, has been refreshed with the casual elegance of a Nantucket Looms home.

The Nantucket Looms design team celebrates the artistic passions of these homeowners—their proclivity for collecting exceptional works of art, antiques, and curios that reflect their family heritage and the natural beauty of the island—to curate a welcoming coastal-styled home. Featured works of art by Julija Mostykanova and Kenneth Layman set the tone for this all-shades-of-blue palette with their abstract landscapes and harbor scenes, reminiscent of the changing seasons and moments on Nantucket. Both Julija and Kenneth are talented painters who have strong ties with the Nantucket Artists Association.

The open-floor concept on the first floor includes a living room, an adjacent sitting room divided by a sliding door crafted from reclaimed barn wood, a winterized porch converted into a dining room, and a kitchen with a breakfast nook that shares a double-sided fireplace. Shiplap walls and ceilings crisscrossed with painted and natural wood beams add texture while giving a nod to Nantucket's maritime past.

In the living room, two curved-back sofas and a black wrought iron bench are central to the luminous setting. Luxurious velvet and patterned linen cushions lend a tactile character to the space. An unexpected glass and acrylic coffee table is styled with appealing and interesting items. The elements of a well-styled coffee table should include layers that are both decorative and functional, such as stacks of books, coasters, a bowl of marbles, a potted plant, and boxes of different sizes that add height. Items that tell a story of the homeowners' interests are always great conversation starters when gathering around the table.

A large painting of a dory boat by Sergio Roffo energizes a corner of the living room with nautical allure, enhancing the connection with the nearby sitting room, where the atmosphere is inspired by Julija's abstract painting of a harbor. A cashmere throw in deep navy,

JULIJA MOSTYKANOVA
PAINTER

Abstract painter Julija Mostykanova said, "Inspiration finds me in the moment, working at my easel in the studio." Once she shows up in the studio, things start to happen. She showed up at Nantucket Looms for the first time about fifteen years ago with her handcrafted decoupage glass paperweights and later on with a few small paintings, marking the beginning of her career as a Nantucket artist. Over time Julija's work has evolved into something more abstract and looser and possessed with the mysterious feeling evoked by the Gray Lady herself. "Julija's work is at home in any house it is displayed in," said Rebecca Jusko Peraner, a partner at Nantucket Looms. "Contemporary or historic, it fits right in. The abstract spatial qualities, color palette, and whimsical brushstrokes she utilizes give life to her art." Born in Lithuania, Julija studied chemistry at the Kaunas University of Technology before she arrived on Nantucket to spend the summer—and never left. A self-taught artist, Julija has always been artsy and crafty—constantly trying new things to find her way in the world of art. During her first year on Nantucket, she took classes at the Artists Association of Nantucket (AAN) where the sale of her first painting renewed faith in her ability. Julija said, "Nantucket is such a supportive community both in terms of fellow artists and collectors. It would be very hard to be a full-time artist elsewhere." She finds it very freeing to paint from memory and said, "I love to attack the canvas" with frenetic energy. The AAN's Artistic Director Bobby Frazier noted Julija is their biggest seller—and "that's a big deal." This is probably because, as Julija said, "when I wake up every day, I can't wait to go to work."

handwoven by Nantucket Looms weavers, adds a tantalizing flourish of color and comfort to this sectional sofa, chosen by the design team to maximize the seating. Roman shades filter sunlight and blend nicely with the shiplap of the walls. Handsome built-in bookcases are styled with the owner's collections of decoys, photographs, and a lightship basket, a long-standing island craft now commonly used as a handbag by women. Works by local artists embellish a corner above a curved built-in banquette in the kitchen that also functions as a window seat. Pottery serving pieces form a centerpiece arrangement on the round table, which is accompanied by two upholstered chairs nestled into the space. A framed photograph by Daniel Sutherland shows the reflection of moonlight on the ocean at night.

A striking mahogany countertop complements the modernist brass and horn cabinet pulls on this well-fitted built-in bar. A painting by Nantucket Looms artist Julie Gifford, whose artwork is inspired by the natural world, and a gold-framed scene enliven the space. A variety of pleated tin planters, candlesticks, trays, and other pieces useful for entertaining adorn this wet bar, replete with ingredients for golden-hour libations. Nearby, a light-filled sitting area is the ideal place to put up your feet, relax, and read the newspaper or a favorite book. It is comfortably furnished with modern, whitewashed open-weave chairs, Moroccan-themed poufs, and a side table featuring a bleached teakwood bowl from Indonesia, adding to the coastal connections.

Beginning with the paint-splattered floor, the four-season porch is layered with patterns in a coastal palette. The understated effect of this painting technique in true Nantucket Looms style elevates the look of the room. The expert fold of the handwoven sky blue throw, accompanied by the blue-and-white hydrangea

PAGES 52-53: In the primary bedroom of the East End house, a four-poster wooden bobbin bed in oyster gray has been placed next to a bone inlay side table that holds a ceramic lamp in soft shades of white on top. PAGES 54-55: A seaside abstract painting by Julija Mostykanova establishes the vibe for Knut House with its all-shades-of-blue palette. Nantucket Harbor, visible from the dining room and second-floor bedrooms, provides nautical inspiration for this artistic abode—from the handcrafted shiplap walls to the coffered ceiling and works of art. OPPOSITE: A sliding barn door provides privacy to the den where the homeowner can work or relax on the sectional sofa below Mostykanova's painting.

ABOVE LEFT: Coasters in a pedestal dish, a book displayed in a decorative tray, as well as objets d'art are elements of a well-styled coffee table. **ABOVE RIGHT**: The owners' collections of shore bird carvings, books, and artwork add interest to this corner bookshelf. Displayed are photographs (clockwise from top left) by Ansel Adams, Daniel Sutherland, Edward Weston, and Alex MacLean. **OPPOSITE**: The dining room, set in the four-season porch, has a view of the harbor. With its splatter-painted floor, wicker dining chairs, and wall paneling that resembles weathered exterior wood, this room embodies seaside cottage charm.

OPPOSITE: A collection of small paintings by British artist Beccy Marshall embellish a corner above a curved built-in banquette, constructed by Scott Bowman of North Atlantic Woodworking. High-performance Thibault fabrics cover the banquette and the dining chairs. A framed photograph by Daniel Sutherland shows the reflection of moonlight on the ocean at night. ABOVE: A well-stocked bar is set up on the countertop of the cabinetry with modernist brass and horn pulls. A painting by Julie Gifford enlivens the space.

OPPOSITE: These white-washed rope chairs provide additional seating in the light-filled sitting room. On the wall hangs a photograph by Sebastião Salgado. ABOVE: A contemporary version of a traditional-style bobbin bed graces the guest suite. A wingback chair is upholstered in a bouclé fabric with a windowpane design used on the throw pillow. On the wall, a vintage hooked rug from the 1940s is on display.

floral artistry created by Nantucket Looms interior designer Brooke Gherardini, expresses the importance of attention to detail. A bobbin bed with a Nantucket Looms handwoven mohair throw, botanical motif pillows, and a bouclé chair, provide extra-special accommodations in the first-floor guest room. On the wall is a vintage hooked rug. An old-fashioned alarm clock tells the time of day.

On the second floor under the eaves of the house's roof, the primary bedroom, with a gorgeous view of the harbor, features finely crafted traditional furnishings and the owners' Moroccan carpet that is the perfect color of blue. Impressive bedside tables wrapped with grasscloth are animated with a painting by Nantucket Looms artist Kenneth Layman.

The cozy hideaway located on the lower level is exceptionally inviting. Double queen-size beds made up in luxurious Italian bed linens add the perfect touch to this guest room. The design team often decorates rooms with limited light sources with bright fun fabrics and rugs as can be seen on the wingback chair. A deep navy mohair throw with silk accent banding, woven in the weaving studio in yarns saturated with color provides the perfect final touch to this room.

LEFT: Continuing the coastal theme throughout the house a nautical color palette of red, white, and blue is used in the lower-level guest bedroom. Two queen-size beds are upholstered in a geometric printed fabric and made up in luxurious Italian percale linens. **ABOVE:** A chair covered in a playful striped fabric fills the corner of the bedroom. The deep navy handwoven mohair throw with its silk accent banding is the final comforting touch.

MOOR JOY

◆

A Coastal
Sanctuary

Decorated with the tasteful artistry of Nantucket Looms and surrounded by the serenity of the island, Moor Joy, formerly a part of the Westmoor Farms Estate, has been a family retreat since the early 1990s. Originally designed by Alan Perkins of Twig Perkins Inc., this house was remodeled later in the 1990s by Chip Webster of Chip Webster Architecture of Nantucket to bring the utopian vision of the former owners to life. A magical place was created where children and adults alike could be carefree.

Today, the residence has been reimagined for twenty-first century living, including the addition of a new kitchen, new floors, and another bedroom. Nantucket Looms has decorated the main house and guest cottage with a classic island vibe, bringing in the outside colors of sand, sea, sky, beachgrass, and dunes. To embrace the architectural beauty and rustic aesthetic of the houses with their marvelous structural beams and painted white shiplap ceilings, a curated balance of pairing the old with the new—a favorite element of Nantucket Looms design—was brought into play. Oversize furniture with an elevated look was selected for its modern appeal and upholstered in high-performance fabrics. The inviting and casual ambiance perfectly suits the active family lifestyle.

To complement the scale of the living room in the main house, a set of sofas was selected for their depth and comfort. Nantucket Looms throws, handwoven in cashmere and alpaca fibers, along with hand-printed and silk-screened cushions and pillows, add layers of sophistication. Continuing the symmetry, two identical rope-textured coffee tables are paired with contemporary wingback chairs.

For home design, the island's seafaring history is always a source of inspiration. Suspended from the vaulted ceiling is an unusual nautical-themed light fixture comprised of handblown glass floats knotted together with rope. The reflection of the bobbin-framed mirror over a cabinet with a painted shagreen finish, brings a quietness of space to the balanced vignette featuring a Susan Bacle sculpture. Adjacent to the living room is a reading area with a round table. A built-in cabinet provides storage for the owner's puzzles and display space for books and favorite objets d'art.

Artwork by Nantucket Looms artists enlivens the dining room space. On the bar shelving are two paintings by Kenneth Layman. Hanging on a nearby wall is a painting by Julija Mostykanova. While the striking blue chairs upholstered in fabric by Peter Dunham take center stage, rustic vintage finials, matched by a pair of

KENNETH LAYMAN
PAINTER

Kenneth Layman has been represented by Nantucket Looms since 1971. "Ken is a true master of his craft," said Bess Clarke. A close friend of both Andy Oates and Bill Euler, Ken said, "They are intertwined in my story because they were a part of it—and still are." After living on Nantucket for over forty years, Ken said the exquisite natural beauty of the island is ever present in his imagination, the well into which he dips his painter's brush to create masterly works in oils on board in the manner of Wassily Kandinsky and Mark Rothko. Drawn to the placement of shapes, line and form, Ken brings bold colors, clean brush strokes, and an exciting sense of movement. The ethereal qualities of his landscapes and cloud scenes bring the wind and sea to life with dune grasses swaying in ocean breezes beneath soft blue skies. Whether an abstract, a large landscape, a small scene, or an antique shaker box lid, "the paintings are all from my mind," Ken said. Describing his intuitive process, he "finds a painting by starting it, knowing it will inevitably become something," believing "if an artist listens to a painting, it will guide their brush." Ken's work Day of the Eclipse has been exhibited in the US Department of State's Arts in the Embassy Program at American Embassies in Athens, Greece; Geneva, Switzerland; São Paulo, Brazil; and in the US Mission to the United Nations in New York City. Ken is a recipient of the Copley Society Air France Award.

PAGES 66–67: Artwork by Nantucket Looms artists enlivens the home's dining room space. On the bar are two paintings by Kenneth Layman. Hanging on a nearby wall is a painting by Julija Mostykanova. The comfortable blue armchairs are upholstered in fabric by Peter Dunham. Rustic vintage finials, matched by a pair of contemporary rattan chandeliers, add interest to the double-pedestal dining room table. A reproduction of a French handkerchief planter is filled with ferns to brighten up the space. PAGES 68–69: The two Layman paintings are examples of his landscape and abstract styles. ABOVE: Susan Bacle's sculpture *Three Fish on Driftwood* is displayed on the shagreen cabinet below the bobbin-framed mirror. RIGHT: To complement the dramatic scale of the living room, an arrangement of sofas and modern wingback chairs is anchored by two coffee tables styled with books and decorative objects that relate to Nantucket's seafaring history.

ABOVE: Inspired by blown-glass fishing floats, this sculptural chandelier is made of handblown glass "bubbles" bound together with knotted rope. **OPPOSITE**: A space for playing games and building puzzles, replete with a marble-topped table surrounded by four upholstered chairs, was created adjacent to the living room. A painting by Adam Umbach hangs in the background.

ABOVE: Departing from the mostly white walls of the home, a leaf-patterned wallpaper was chosen to make this dressing room stand out. An oversized upholstered bench in a joyful fabric was selected to bring character to the space. **OPPOSITE:** Barbara Clarke's photograph *Seafoam* adds depth to the space above an upholstered white linen bed with navy blue welting in the main house. It is flanked by navy wooden inlay bedside tables. A white chevron wool rug brings comfort underfoot. **FOLLOWING PAGES:** A close-up view of the bedroom's details and Clarke's photograph, which was taken of the south shore of the island. Large-scale botanical-printed Euro pillows and an embroidered ivory lumbar pillow with navy blue knotted welting are the finishing touches.

chandeliers positioned directly overhead, bring focus to the double-pedestal dining room table.

In a bedroom in the main house, a Barbara Clarke photograph of the surf adds luster to the space over the bed. The blue-and-white theme with pillows, a painted wood bedside table, the white chevron rug, a pouf, and shutters on the windows adds a fresh feeling to the space.

Playing off the whimsy of the living room in the guest cottage, a vibrant red, white, and blue theme can be found. Anchoring the room is a large white sectional sofa with bench-seat cushions and two oversized white swivel chairs, all in high-performance fabrics.

In the tradition of many Nantucket homes, this property has been reconfigured and reimagined, but the original purpose of creating a haven thirty miles from the mainland still can be found.

BARBARA CLARKE
PHOTOGRAPHER

Nantucket Looms proudly represents a roster of over seventy artists, and Barbara Clarke, an accomplished photographer, is one of them. "There is a mystical quality to Barbara's photography," said Rebecca Jusko Peraner, a Nantucket Looms partner. "The way she captures the golden hour and her use of light bring a sense of serenity to her work." Especially in the off-season, the tranquil and isolated beauty of the beaches are Barbara's muse—Cisco, Fat Ladies, and Nobadeer—are mere steps away from her front door. At the insistence of her brother, John Keane, she left their homeland of Ireland during her college years to spend a summer on what he had described to her as "this amazing place called Nantucket." She came for the summer—and returned the following April with her childhood sweetheart to make their home on the island. Barbara is a trained jeweler and basket weaver but today focuses on photography. With a camera by her side, she seeks to capture the special moments in life—a laugh or a reflective light crossing the horizon at sunset—artful reminders of the beauty and joy of Nantucket. Finding inspiration in the ethereal effects of the island, such as the fog and the crashing waves, surrounding moments for her become magical. In fact, her photography is often mistaken for a painting. It brings a smile and sense of deep satisfaction when people tell Barbara they bought one of her "paintings" at an auction. Even though she hasn't chosen to dab at a canvas with a brush, it's fair to say she paints with the lens of a camera.

LEFT: The sitting room adjacent to the primary bedroom suite is comfortably furnished with two chairs upholstered in an ikat fabric. The contemporary suede desk is styled with a leather chair. The painting on the wall between the windows is by Nantucket Looms artist Gay Held. Grass wallpaper dresses the walls. **FOLLOWING PAGES:** A variety of textures can be seen in this bedroom. Rope handles embellish the chest of drawers, and the lamps are white-washed wicker. The bed features a tufted linen headboard with Euro pillows in a boucle fabric. A kelp green handwoven cashmere throw is draped across the king-size bed. To keep consistency between the two rooms, the same light fixtures of painted rattan are used, and the walls are covered in grass wallpaper.

RIGHT: Playing off the whimsical shape of the living room in the guest cottage— a space used for hosting visitors of all ages—a vibrant red, white, and blue theme can be found. Anchoring the room are a large white sectional sofa with bench-seat cushions and two oversized white swivel chairs, all covered in high-performance fabrics. Silk-screened throw pillows add the finishing touch. A painting by Megan Hinton is displayed on the coffee table.

CARRIAGE HOUSE

---◆---

Ode to Modernism

Fortunately, thanks to astute, modern attitudes in support of historic preservation on Nantucket, the saving of the Carriage House in Nantucket's historic downtown district has become a familiar story. Originally built as a barn and servant's quarters, the wood-frame structure was one of several outbuildings used in the service of a brick Georgian-style mansion built by Henry Coffin in 1834. At some point the barn was converted to a carriage house.

Organizations such as the Historic District Commission (HDC) were created to preserve historic buildings and to protect the character of the community. Eugenie Voorhees, a former owner of the Carriage House, served as chairwoman of the HDC. In 2000, alarmed by increasing levels of real estate development threatening the architectural integrity of the island, Voorhees and members of the Historic District Commission had Nantucket included on the list of the eleven "Most Endangered Places" in the nation in an effort to bring national recognition to the situation. In an article written by Noelle Barton in the *Cape Cod Times* in 2000 Voorhees described this designation as an "opportunity to recognize that we have problems and to work on solutions to solve them. A lot of these things can be undone. There can be an educational process on the island to turn the tide." Voorhees was miffed at the perceived excess of the island newcomers. In an article by Tom Congdon in *Nantucket Nouveau* in 1999, Voorhees humorously complained, "These new people don't share bathrooms. There's got to be one per person, each as big as a normal bedroom."

Voorhees, who died in 2018, "was a great friend of Bill and Andy's," said Liz Winship. "She had a great design

PAGES 84–85: The Josef Albers's print and handwoven Nantucket Looms cashmere throw complement the exterior Nantucket Blue color of the shutters and doors of this house. The sofas, upholstered with a traditional linen/cotton plain woven tabby fabric in natural taupe, are arranged around a central coffee table featuring a glass sculpture by Massimo Micheluzzi. The spray of orchids is an homage to architect Hugh Newell Jacobsen, who designed this home in the 1980s for Eugenie Voorhees, who had chaired the Nantucket Historic District Commission. **OPPOSITE**: A minimalist style is in keeping with the modern elegance of the rooms (clockwise from top left): The galley-style kitchen is efficient with its high-quality appliances. The woven chair in the entry is by Gareth Neal. A simple, understated design prevails in the living room. A nod to surrealism, the Finn Juhl Pelican Chair with sheepskin upholstery sits in the primary bedroom. **ABOVE**: The framed black-and-white prints *12 Views for Caroline Tatyana* are by Brice Marden. They add a beguiling backdrop to the white handwoven upholstery by Nantucket Looms.

ABOVE: A tabletop built-in desk beneath two corner windows creates a light-filled workspace. RIGHT: A prominent feature in the dining room is the wall of bookcases designed by Hugh Newell Jacobsen, who remodeled the house for the previous owner. He called it his egg-crate design.

sense of how the house was to look and used a lot of the textiles from the Looms, including Oates's acclaimed linen and ramie fabric." In 1984 Voorhees bought a typical Nantucket two-and-one-half-story house on Orange Street and undertook an extensive renovation with Washington, D.C., architect Hugh Newell Jacobsen, who was prized for his refined sense of modernity, execution of clean lines, light-filled interiors, and signature egg-crate bookcases.

While the island's housing trend was supersizing, Voorhees downsized. In 2002 she exchanged the Orange Street house for a two-bedroom, two-and-a-half-bath carriage house, working once again with Jacobsen to transform her new abode into one of the trendiest houses on the island. Together they conjured a haven of solitude

with an all-white light-filled interior featuring a library/ dining room combination with floor-to-ceiling egg-crate bookcases. Jacobsen explained, "You are always taking books off the shelves and the rest all fall down . . . With this design you can remove a whole foot and they won't." The original full-height barn doors, off-sided shutters, and peaked ceilings were retained in keeping with Jacobsen's creed that "good architecture never shouts. It is like a well-mannered lady, kind to its neighbors. It takes a double take to know that she is there at all." In 2003 the Voorhees-Jacobsen project received the Award of Excellence in Architecture from the American Institute of Architects, Washington, D.C., chapter. By the end of Voorhees's life, the cottage had fallen into a state of

HILLARY ANAPOL
RUG WEAVER

Hillary Anapol, the daughter of a third-generation textile family, learned the traditional art of Swedish and Scandinavian rug weaving as an apprentice to world-renowned master weaver Margaretta Nettles of Eskilstuna, Sweden. Nettles trained in textile design at Stockholm's State School of Art and Design, which today is called Konstfack University of Arts, Crafts and Design. In the late 1970s Nettles moved to Nantucket where she opened her own studio on Union Street and taught the art of weaving to students, including Hillary. At this time, Nettles also collaborated with then Nantucket Looms owner Liz Winship on the design of bespoke tapestries and rugs for the store's clients. Since 1998 Hillary has been the proprietor of Nantucket Weaver, a rug-weaving studio on the island where she continues to create heirloom-quality, flat-weave, or reversible rag rugs in cotton and linen fabrics and wool and tapestry rugs in linen and wool yarns. Working on twelve-foot-wide looms, Hillary, who works alone, has developed a modern interpretation of the traditional methods of Swedish rug-making techniques as well as an expertise in color blending. Her rugs are finished with a solid edge on both sides that never unravels. Hillary recognizes that while weaving techniques will remain the same, taste, color, and design keep changing as home interiors are updated. Hillary especially enjoys welcoming homeowners, interior designers, and architects to her studio to guide them in the design of their one-of-a-kind rugs, in the selection of colors and fabric, and in determining the right size rug to anchor the furniture and complement a space.

disrepair, and the current owners painstakingly restored it. The owners, who had been friendly with Voorhees, and whose apartment in Washington, D.C. was designed by Jacobsen, chose to stay true to the Jacobsen spirit and make the least amount of disturbance; only the heating system was updated.

In the heart of the home, you will find the best examples of Nantucket Looms craftsmanship. Rebecca Jusko Peraner, who with her team wove the fabrics by hand for this home, described the new owners as "connoisseurs of fine art and impeccable craftsmanship, evident by the collections on display in their home." The sofa is covered in a traditional linen/cotton, plain-woven tabby fabric in natural taupe, letting the beautiful yarns and furniture lines of the sofa speak.

The fabric on the window bench seats is an ivory cotton slub canvas fabric and one that the Nantucket Looms weavers have woven for many installations—sofas, seats, pillows, walls, and even fabric bags. The slub is the element that takes it beyond a basic canvas. Using a basket weave makes the scale of the texture more pronounced and the simple ivory fabric more interesting. The fabric on the Flex Form custom one-arm chairs is Rebecca's interpretation of Andy Oates's linen and ramie fabric. It is created with a mercerized sewing thread woven in a basket-weave structure alternating a thick pic of yarn with a thinner pic to create the ribbed fabric. Pic is a weaving term used to describe the singular horizontal yarn or weft thread. The mercerized cotton thread used in the warp is strong and has a delicate sheen to it that mimics the ramie used in the original fabric. Rebecca added that "using linen in this interpretation ensures durability."

Throughout the day, the terrace beckons inquiring eyes. The understated elegance of the garden surrounded by privet hedges ensures this hidden gem in the center of town will never be discovered.

OPPOSITE: The floor of the guest room is covered with a hand-woven rag rug in a tabby pattern created by Hillary Anapol. The homeowners painted the permanent structural pole a shade of red to contrast with the blue-and-white color scheme.
FOLLOWING PAGES: Originally a horse barn, the carriage house doors open to a welcoming terrace surrounded by an English country-style garden designed by Katie Hemingway. The flower beds are filled with plants that bloom throughout the season. The tall privet hedge affords privacy from the street, enabling the barn-size doors to remain open to the refreshing island breezes.

OUTBACK

◆

A Hosting
Haven

On a quiet dead-end street on the edge of town, and hidden behind a high privet hedge, is a picturesque modern interpretation of a classic Nantucket cottage that was built in 2021. It's the kind of place one falls in love with at first sight and hopes to never leave. This cottage is called OutbACK, with an emphasis on ACK, the Federal Aviation Administration's abbreviation for the Nantucket Memorial Airport. Nantucket Looms Interior Design Studio has brought the artful design of their coastal style to this guesthouse cottage with agreeable results.

After working with the homeowners on their main house also on this property, the Nantucket Looms interiors team was asked to design the cottage. Being a part of the process from the very beginning allowed the team to provide their guidance on all aspects of the project including fixtures, finishes, paint selections, and decor. A cottage for all seasons, it's as comfortable and inviting in February as it is in August. It has a welcoming front porch and a beautiful backyard. The best part of this cottage is when it fills up with family and friends visiting for special island celebrations: Daffodil Weekend in the springtime, the not-to-be-missed Annual Nantucket Christmas Stroll, and the many happy occasions of birthdays and anniversaries.

The tidy well-manicured lawn that surrounds a terrace of flat irregular-shaped stone—a lovely summertime setting for dining under the stars—leads to the welcoming open-concept space ideal for entertaining and reflective of island living. A bevy of plump pillows in interesting patterns and stripes, along with a collection of handwoven throws, are spread across cushioned

PAGES 94–95: The covered porch beneath the shingled gable is the perfect transition space between the terraced lawn and this house. On Nantucket, the pitch of a roof line must be consistent with the Nantucket Historic District Commission's guidelines. RIGHT: The open-floor plan of the living room, dining room, and kitchen lends itself to a welcoming entertaining atmosphere.

ABOVE: The built-in bar is styled with must-have accoutrements for entertaining. The bar wall, which is constructed of oak, has a herringbone pattern that adds architectural interest. OPPOSITE: A light-blue-and-white theme prevails in the primary bedroom with the handwoven throw, framed artwork, and draperies. The height of the canopy bed draws the eye to the cathedral oak ceiling.

seating. The room is accented with organic elements, including the jute rug in the seating area, the root bowl on the kitchen counter, and the whitewashed oak chevron-patterned backsplash at the bar, all of which enhance the beauty of the light-filled space. The open-weave rattan lounge chairs and counter stools bring allure and a refined sense of well-being to the coastal ambiance.

The relaxed look continues to the guest suites on the second floor. The primary suite is layered with soothing shades of color and texture. The neutral base wall color showcases a striking canopy bed dressed with gorgeous bed linens, and a bounty of comfortable pillows in coordinating patterns and colors. The soft blue hue of the draperies, beautiful wool carpet, and upholstered chair add elegance to the space. The contrasting shape of the contemporary lamp on the side table adds a surprising lightness of touch.

Soft-hued organic elements are segued into the secondary suite with the woven seagrass headboard, fresh flowers, and sea urchin objet d'art. The lacquered side table next to the bed blends seamlessly with the handwoven throw draped effortlessly across the pristine bed linens.

The large outdoor shower constructed of cedar, a tradition on Nantucket, is a favorite feature of the house—especially in summertime when the sprays of water are tinged with colors of the rainbow. A collection of plush towels, a handy stool to sit on, ship cleats used for hooks, an improv collection of shells and stones, an antique sieve, and luxurious bath and beauty products complete the furnishing of this plein-air space.

Whether one is returning from a glorious day on the water, at the beach, or simply visiting from the mainland, the inspiring coastal style of this cottage hidden behind the hedge is sure to please in every season of the year.

RIGHT: A shiplap wall with a woven lampakanay rope bed and a lacquered linen-wrapped bedside table gives this guest room a cozy and rustic look and continues the house's light blue-and-white palette. Shiplap was originally used to waterproof ships. The boards are cut with an overlapping effect for extra strength and durability.

JEFF DIVINE | SEVENTIES SURF PHOTOGRAPHS

OPPOSITE: An outdoor space ready for entertaining on the terraced lawn, which is adjacent to the covered porch. Vases filled with fresh-picked flowers add to the inviting atmosphere. ABOVE: A must-have on Nantucket today is an outdoor shower, which assures sand stays outside. This is often treated not just as a place to wash off but as another room of the house to display collections found at the beach.

RANTUM SCOOTING

---◆---

A Hidden Gem

The worldly-wise elements of Nantucket Looms refined style elevates the East-Coast-meets-West-Coast vibe of Rantum Scooting. Brimming with the timeless appeal of a house by the sea it is located within easy walking distance of the excitement and energy of the old town and harbor. The muted color palette, the eclectic and curious personal collections, and themes of seafaring culture enrich this house. It is the most wondrous home to return to after a random scoot, or leisurely walk, around the island, as the name of the house in an old Nantucket dialect suggests. As you approach the home, full-size boxwoods line the path that extends to the guest cottage and back garden. This building has an amazing history. In the late twentieth century, it was the home of American author, journalist, and Pulitzer Prize winner David Halberstam, his wife, Jean, and their daughter, Julia Sandness Halberstam, as well as a favorite gathering place for literary lights. If only walls could talk. Halberstam dedicated his book, *Summer of '49*, about the pennant race between the New York Yankees and the Boston Red Sox, to his friends—Nantucket Looms founders Andy Oates and Bill Euler.

An impressive and mature fiery red Japanese Maple tree adorns the Greek Revival exterior entrance. After the Great Fire of 1846 when approximately one-third of the town was destroyed, houses were rebuilt in the Greek Revival manner, the prevailing style of the day. What makes this residence so special is its similarity to a Quaker meeting house, which gives the oversized main room a spiritual and peaceful feeling. The floor-to-ceiling window allows ample light to stream through

PAGES 104–105: This four-season porch located next to the kitchen is an intimate space to enjoy a roaring fire or a breezy summer afternoon. ABOVE: The portrait of this island seaman by Doug Brega is hung on a wall of shiplap in this light-filled corner with an ornate collection of walking sticks displayed nearby. OPPOSITE: Beneath the open-raftered ceiling, a long communal dining table holds a hand-woven basket filled with green plants. The doors open to the porch beyond.

RIGHT: A colorful aquatint by Joan Miró, *Le Cosmonaute*, fills a corner of this warm and inviting sitting room designed in a palette of soft whites with contrasting organic hues of gray, black, and brown. FOLLOWING PAGES: The front entry of the house opens to a cathedral-ceiling Quaker-style living room. The central focus is the large window with its light-filled views of the garden flanked by Henry Moore etchings. Objects gathered from the owner's travels are grouped with green plants between two textured lamps.

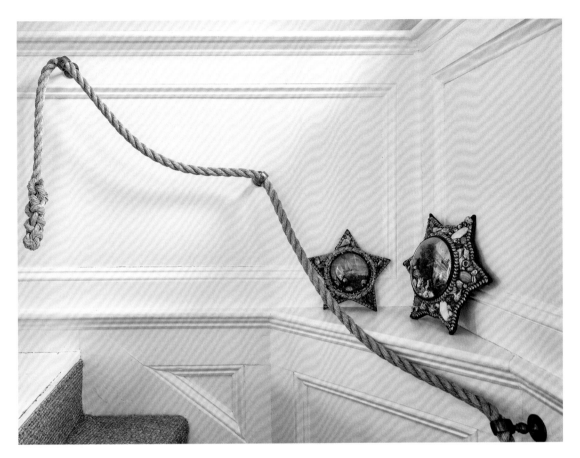

OPPOSITE: A fireside sitting area is embellished with the owner's favorite collection of shells, along with a star-shaped item known as a sailor's valentine, which is a sentimental form of shell craft. A Henry Moore etching hangs next to the fireplace.
ABOVE: A repurposed rope serves as a handrail on the staircase leading to the second floor. A corner shelf is decorated with two star-shaped sailor's valentines.

with expansive views to the front yard. The family enjoys spending time in this room playing games, reading, and sitting by the fireplace. Tucked away at the corner of the room is a staircase one can use to access the overlooking balcony and second-floor bedrooms. Found throughout the house are the homeowners' sentimental and cherished collections, including seashells, vintage sand pails, and walking sticks.

As one meanders into the back part of the house, the spaces become more intimate and relaxed. A comfortable sectional sofa in the den with oversize linen pillows is a perfect place to read a book or take a nap. The dining room, which opens to the kitchen, accommodates a long, narrow dining table with slipcover linen chairs, ideal for hosting large gatherings of friends. An all-season enclosed porch can be found off the dining room with seagrass furniture, a modern organic coffee table by Blaxsand, a company whose products are sourced from Indonesia and made of reclaimed or sustainable materials, a driftwood sculpture, and a reclaimed wooden mantel, providing additional space to enjoy the company of loved ones.

Functional spaces such as a butler's pantry and mudroom have been turned into areas with charm and interest. Homes can be places where a person hangs a hat and goes to sleep or a place like Rantum Scooting, where the spirit of the island is honored.

ABOVE: A bar ready for coffee service displays the owner's collection of silver utensils and serving pieces. The painting is by the homeowner's friend Mary Morant. RIGHT: A portrait of a serious-faced gentleman by an anonymous artist overlooks the beer taps, where Nantucket's own Cisco Beer is being served.

OPPOSITE: A window seat furnished in comforting shades of blue is the perfect space to relax while gazing at the garden. **ABOVE**: A guest room with a view is furnished with full-size beds dressed in luxurious linens. A lamp with a sea-urchin-inspired base sits atop the table and illuminates nighttime reading. A reproduction milking stool is kept close. **FOLLOWING PAGES**: The walkway lined with mature boxwood shrubs leads to the guest house and the back of the property, where there is a terrace and koi pond.

WINSHIP'S MONOHANSETT

◆

A Curator's Compound

Liz Winship is one of Nantucket Island's leading ladies—one with a keen eye who was at the helm of Nantucket Looms for forty-three years. It's an extraordinary opportunity to visit the home of Liz and Todd Winship to experience her vibrant spirit of place and learn how she makes a house a home, to see where she kicks off her shoes and entertains her guests, to admire her collections, and to be inspired by her coastal style. Monohansett is part of a family compound: a beehive of activity with grandsons, daughters, and sons-in-law, who are always on the go. Their two daughters, Bess and Claire, reside with their husbands and children on the family property as well. The house is named for Monohansett Island, a name of Native American origin, and one of the Elizabeth Islands located in the town of Gosnold, Massachusetts.

The organic architecture of this Spanish plantation-style house, a basic U-shape, atypical for Nantucket, was designed by Mark Poor of MWP Design and built in 1998. This unusual shingle-style home was influenced by the designs of Frank Lloyd Wright, the legendary American architect. It was adapted to modern life on Nantucket with its low horizontal roof line—twenty-one feet at the highest peak—open floor plan, and connected light-filled interior and exterior spaces, as well as the fine interior woodworking finishes by Todd Winship. This all ensures that the house blends seamlessly with the surrounding landscape. The leisurely sophistication of the house makes it perfect for entertaining. The expansive kitchen opens into the central courtyard finished with mahogany decking—an oasis for al fresco dining with ready access to the saltwater pool, which is a big part

PAGES 120–121: On the table beneath the window overlooking the courtyard is an eclectic assortment of objects of interest, including tribal pieces found by Liz and Todd Winship while on safari in Botswana; tops of lightning rods from barns in Pennsylvania; and works of art, among them an early Robert W. Stark III painting, at left, featuring a nectarine, and a porcelain piece by Mara Superior displayed with a ship pulley. To the right, a stone fruit collection is displayed near an art deco lamp. On the wood floor are a French yellowware bowl and a star-shaped architectural support used to hold building trusses. At right is a partial view of an Orkney chair that was handcrafted from local materials in Orkney, an archipelago in Scotland. LEFT: In the entryway, oyster sticks, once used to cultivate oysters, are propped against a side wall next to a vintage hooked rug. On the scrubbed pine server is a late 1800s ship diorama and two Victorian raku balls handcrafted by Constance Leslie of Providence, Rhode Island. Found on Nantucket, the diorama is a premium piece of American folk art, with its original fringe, flags, and hand-painted symbols. To the right is a mahogany Victorian child's correction chair, designed to fix faulty posture in children, with a woven cane seat. Lightning rods with a beautiful patina hang above it. On the panel wall in the hallway is an oil painting by Leigh Palmer that Liz inherited from Andy and Bill.

ABOVE: In the dining room, a folk art collection of Mark McNair hand-carved shorebirds, which are seasonal to the island, are grouped together on a side wall. A framed red sail oil painting by Robert Stark Jr. is displayed on a credenza next to a 1930s chip-carving, or tramp-art, frame on the wall. **RIGHT:** A vintage large cod fish market sign enjoys a commanding presence in the light-filled living room. A bowl containing a marble fruit collection is displayed on a side table at left. On the other side table is a group of three handblown glass dories in a glass case, made by Marc Petrovic, that Liz found at Dane Gallery on Centre Street in Nantucket. As a final flourish, the outline of the island is etched on the outside.

of the families' lives. Over the last twenty-five years the Winships have established an arboretum through their tradition of planting trees, such as pear and apple among the grasses and succulents, where they celebrate special occasions.

In the house, a V-grooved, knot-free pine paneling was used for the cathedral ceiling that shelters both the front entryway and centrally located living room, which are separated by a partial wall. At particular times of day, beams of natural light streak like shooting stars through a dormer window positioned above the front door and across the living room ceiling to a wall of windows that reveals the adjacent courtyard. The opening of these sight lines extends interior views, enhancing the feeling of spaciousness.

Liz adheres to Nantucket Looms philosophy of mixing the old and new, the elegant with the whimsical,

MARK McNAIR
DECOY ARTIST

Nantucket Island is a stopover on the Atlantic Flyway for migrating birds. Another one is a small farm located on the water and salt marshes in Craddockville, Virginia, on the Eastern Shore. This is where preeminent master American woodcarver Mark McNair creates nontraditional decoys in an abstract style, more as an art form instead of as a tool for hunters. Mark, who originally showed his work at Nantucket Looms, specializes in waterfowl and shorebird decoys, weathervanes, and related folk art. Mark initially fell under the spell of woodcarving while on a boating excursion on Long Island Sound and remembers "hearing the whistle of wigs. [hooded mergansers, a species of small ducks] and these ducks coming out of the fog and glimpsing them for a moment so fast. They were two drakes and a hen, and they turned and displayed their sides and bellies, then were gone." And, when introduced to the art of decoys, he quickly took to the craft. While carving, Mark looks for patterns and works to define the waterfowl movement. He works with cedar and paints with oil to capture the finer details of feathers and the intricate textures of each decoy. The bottom of each piece bears Mark's hand-carved signature. Mark's work is held in public and private collections that include the Shelburne Museum in Vermont, the Historic de Witt Cottage in Virginia Beach, and the Ward Museum of Wildfowl Art in Salisbury, Maryland.

the sleek with the cozy. Taking a cue from the homes of the whalers who displayed their exotic and unusual treasures from around the world with the plainer Quaker style of furniture, she mixes more recent Billy Baldwin pieces with quirky finds from Nantucket's Take It or Leave It, also known as Madaket Mall. Earth tones of greens, inspired by a corner cupboard painted by island artist Johanna Paulsen-Kane, and hues of yellow and orange featured in the surrounding landscape echo throughout the interior space, a time capsule filled with treasures collected over a lifetime of experiences. It can be said that friendship is at the core of the owner's collections. Take for example, the miniature lightship and rare nesting baskets, gifted to Liz by William "Doc" Magee, the chief chemist for the FBI who had retired to Nantucket and taken up basket weaving. Then, there's the collection of hand-carved birds by Mark McNair, the varied Day of the Dead skeletons, and sweet Mother ceramics presented by Bill Euler, who lovingly nicknamed Liz "Mother."

Another family tradition takes place towards the evening, when the family gathers to reflect on their day, keep an eye on the grandsons swimming in the pool, and watch the glorious sunsets over Nantucket's western sky.

PAGE 126: Displayed in a niche of shelves between the living and dining rooms are two Crown of Thorns frames, showcasing the art of chip-carving, and an assortment of miniature lightship baskets by the late William "Doc" Magee, along with Liz Winship's whimsical collection of curiosities. PAGE 127: A close-up view of the miniature baskets handwoven by Magee, who personally inscribed one: "You made it real. Thanks, Liz"—an acknowledgment that she greatly appreciated. RIGHT: On top of the Knoll glass coffee table is an antique architectural object in the shape of a star. It was used for structural support in the building of a barn. A big iron rod was run through the middle of a beam at each end of the barn and anchored in place with two stars on either side. Also displayed are a fossilized whalebone, a mahogany ditty box created by Mark Sutherland, an assortment of folk art, and hand-carved, stone and macramé balls in a handwoven lightship basket.

PREVIOUS PAGES: A Japanese maple brings a contrast of color to a meadow of grasses surrounding the saltwater pool. A nearby cottage is crowned with a hip roof. ABOVE: A sculpture balanced with rocks and metal moves with the wind in the garden by the pool. OPPOSITE: A collection of vintage glass insulators lines a shelf above the potting table. An Eastern European stone trough is seen below.

EAST END

◆

A 'Sconset
Getaway

The drive to the village of 'Sconset, although only seven miles, brings visitors into a world of their own. Each year thousands of bulbs are planted along the Milestone Road, blooming in time for the Annual Nantucket Daffodil Festival, where dozens of antique cars are paraded to the village for a tailgate picnic. For those who live in 'Sconset, everything they need can be found at the 'Sconset Market, the Chanticleer Restaurant, and Claudette's Sandwich Shop.

The Wampanoags named this far-flung outpost on the edge of the new world, Siasconset, which means "place of bones." The name was later shortened to 'Sconset. As the whaling days commenced, the wigwams, or wetus, were replaced by the whale crews with rows of one-room shacks built side by side along the high bluff with expansive views of the Atlantic Ocean. More importantly for the whalers, the fishing was excellent, and the migrating whales could be monitored with ease. Later on, the one-room shacks were converted to cottages with multiple rooms to shelter fishermen, artists, and actors as they began to flock to this quaint village. Small additions, called "warts," were added to the cottages along with pretty flower-filled postage stamp-size gardens, porches, and picket fences—all wreathed in roses, bringing sweet aromas and charm to the village.

The bright light of springtime and a selection of colors from Nantucket Looms island palette echo throughout the cherished home called East End near 'Sconset's village center—a house that reflects the fun and happy vibe of the owner. Throughout the house the Nantucket Looms design team used hues of blues and greens and accessorized it with collections of things that are meaningful to

PREVIOUS PAGES: A kaleidoscope butterfly print adorns a wall in the dining room at East End. A bouquet of blooming lilies becomes the center of attention on the navy lacquered bobbin leg table. An apple green handwoven cotton throw has been casually draped over a classic-style wicker dining chair. **ABOVE:** The client's vintage dishes are placed on seagrass chargers with Nantucket Looms pinstriped cotton napkins. **OPPOSITE:** A ceramic backsplash in a herringbone pattern enhances the look of the open-concept shelving where a variety of serving pieces are displayed. Woven leather counter stools round out the all-white kitchen.

the homeowner. Recognizing that the first impression of a home is made before you walk in, the Looms is always keeping an eye out for interesting planters and urns as a way to dress up an entryway or back patio.

In the living room two sofas are placed near the center of the room for ease of conversation. They are topped with plump patterned cushions in the blues and greens of 'Sconset. A special chair by the fireplace is the modern version of a traditional bobbin chair and can be pulled up when additional seating is needed. The Nantucket Looms style always includes small tables carefully placed in a sitting area to hold a drink, an interesting object, or a book. The waterfall-edged coffee table is crafted of English pine. Plants and greenery create interesting displays. A large painting with images of the sand, sea, and sky in

JULIE GIFFORD
PAINTER

For Julie Gifford, Nantucket is home—her sweet spot—the place where she met her husband, raised their family, and where she finds creative inspiration. The whimsical nature of her work is sparked by the joy she finds in the natural world of the island, particularly birds and marine life, and in objets d'arts, such as vases of flowers, bowls of fruit, and culinary tools organized into light-hearted compositions that reflect beauty in everyday life. "Julie's versatile use of color, varieties of composition, and shapes make her one of our most dynamic artists," said Bess Clarke of Nantucket Looms. "We are always excited when she arrives at the shop to see her newest creations." Julie is inspired by the push and pull of creativity, incorporating the element of surprise, and she is open to experimentation. She doesn't render her subjects traditionally or adhere to one way of doing things. As a painting progresses, she welcomes the continuous evolution of ideas and finds the unexpected results exciting. Painting in oils, she works in the abstract portraying her subject matter. For Julie, the use of negative space is just as important as positive space because it supports her juxtaposition of shapes, such as arcs, curves, and ovals stacked against squares, with hope that the viewer will enjoy a meaningful experience. Julie studied at the Instituto Allende, San Miguel de Allende, Mexico, and the Center for Creative Studies, Detroit, Michigan. She holds a BFA from Denison University, Granville, Ohio. Julie is the founder and instructor of Julie Gifford Workshops as well as a member of the Cotuit Center for the Arts. Selected works are held in private collections.

beachy tones is placed over the contemporary fireplace as a focal point. The shiplap-covered ceilings add textural elements. Beautiful draperies filter the harsh rays of sunlight and create a soothing backdrop. In a corner, Nantucket Looms designers create a statement with an attractive arrangement of Asian jugs atop a bookcase. The living room includes an informal dining room where 'Sconset-style wicker chairs surround a wood table crafted with bobbin accents. On the wall is a digitized photograph of butterflies in shades of blue, a symbol of hope and happiness that the homeowner enjoys.

In this corner of the kitchen, the feeling is light and airy and dazzles with its view of the outdoors. It's the perfect space to enjoy a cup of tea while working on a favorite puzzle. A painting by Julie Gifford brightens the corner, and island artist Susan Bacle's collection of hand-carved wooden fish echoes the life of the sea. The sleek galley kitchen models efficiency with open shelving and hidden storage space. The fun-colored dishes, artwork, and wooden pieces complement the modern styling. Upstairs, three bedrooms live in a quiet and companionable silence. The primary bedroom features a custom-made Hillary Anapol handwoven cotton and linen rag rug that accents the quiet neutral shades of oyster, cream, ivory, and white.

The first guest room includes a vibrant play on the Nantucket colors of the "Gray Lady" and "Nantucket Red," two island favorites—both of which continue the whimsical and happy theme of the house's decor. The cashmere throw, handwoven by the Nantucket Looms weavers, adds a luxurious finish in the perfect shade of red. In the second guest room, a handsome wall sconce minimizes clutter on the small bedside table. In the lower-level bedroom is a set of built-in bunk beds crafted with handy storage. These homeowners love to host family and friends for the weekend. These welcoming spaces provide an inviting getaway.

PREVIOUS PAGES: In the living room, the coastal hues featured in the painting by Julija Mostykanova are echoed in the blue pillows covered in a handwoven Schumacher fabric and green pillows made with a silk-screened fabric by Peter Fasano. A rustic pine waterfall coffee table is set in the center of the space. OPPOSITE: In the sitting room, the Eero Saarinen tulip dining table is surrounded by chairs upholstered in Lee Industries high-performance fabric. A Boston fern adds a pop of freshness atop a rope-wrapped plant stand.

PREVIOUS PAGES: A shiplap wall lends a nautical touch to this guest bedroom. The abstract painting by Julija Mostykanova embraces the vibrant red accent colors of the room, including the handwoven cashmere throw in the color known as "Faraway Red" at Nantucket Looms. A rope reading lamp dangles over a comfortable wingback chair. **ABOVE AND RIGHT:** The blue-and-white Nantucket poster, a Giclee print reproduced from a paper collage created by artist Liz Roache, enhances the corner of this bunk room. The maritime theme continues with the shiplap wall, navy blue whale's tail sculpture, and circular rope porthole-shaped mirror.

CACHALOT

◆

A Collector's
Paradise

Perched atop a hill on the north shore of Nantucket Island, overlooking the sound, stands a house called Cachalot, the name for the largest of the toothed whales. Situated in the highly desirable Cliff area neighborhood, it is in close proximity to the beautiful Tupancy walking trails. To reach the front of the house via the sturdy plank door with its batten-down-the-hatches look is to traverse time. The architecture is respectful of Nantucket building traditions and harmonizes with that of the Nantucket founders' houses that once stood nearby at Capaum Pond. This home, which was built in the early twenty-first century, was designed to have a rustic yet natural look with an Old World feeling.

A resident of San Francisco in the winter, the owner recruited her West Coast designer, Chantal Lamberto,

PAGE 146: The owner and Todd Stout designed the obelisk tuteur, a symbol of the sun god Ra in Egyptian mythology, for a garden bed filled with annuals and perennials. This focal point gives the garden year-round structure and supports climbing plants. PAGE 147: A framed contemporary lithograph by Christopher Brown hangs above the side table. Two potted myrtle topiaries bookend an assortment of the client's collection of handcrafted Shaker boxes. The antique stool is covered in a Rogers and Goffigon linen fabric. ABOVE: Peering through the metal arch cloaked with pole beans, one can see the gardens and the espaliered flowering crab apple tree in the background. A terra-cotta pot is nestled in a bed of lavender. The white teak obelisk tuteur is covered with cherry tomatoes. OPPOSITE: From the screened-in porch, the dining room can be seen as well as the kitchen window, which was added as a filter for sunlight. The floor was made with reclaimed wood from Pennsylvania, found by the builder of the house, Lindsay Custom Builders. The porch features a vintage wicker chair draped with a Nantucket Looms haze blue handwoven cashmere throw. Antique copper onion lanterns flank the door.

CHILDREN
AT
PLAY

and island contractor, Lindsay Custom Builders, to create this home. She is an avid collector and long-time patron of Nantucket Looms, and Cachalot is a testament to her dedication to garnering local artwork and traditional island crafts and antiques, many of which were found at the shop.

SUSAN BOARDMAN
EMBROIDERER

Susan Boardman's connection to Nantucket Looms began twenty years before she walked into 16 Main Street to show Liz Winship her first embroidered narratives that portrayed the colorful lives of Nantucket women. After graduating from the University of Massachusetts at Amherst in 1968, she studied the art of embroidery at Mary Ann Beinecke's Nantucket School of Needlery Home-Study Extension Course in 1969 and participated in a Nantucket Needlework Seminar with Erica Wilson, an expert embroiderer, in 1974. In the 1960s Mary Anne Beinecke, with her husband, Walter Beinecke Jr., laid the groundwork for continuing this art on Nantucket with Nantucket Looms. Through embroidered narrative, Susan celebrates the stories of one-hundred-and-twenty notable Nantucket women, who over the last four centuries contributed to the vibrancy of their island community. After moving to Nantucket in 1989, Susan said she discovered a rich cache of journals, letters, and diaries of these women in the Nantucket Historical Association's archives and, intrigued by their stories, began what became a twenty-five-year quest not only to unravel their hidden stories but to express them in embroidered narrative. Susan stitched with cotton embroidery floss and used only three types of embroidery stitches: French knot, split stitch, and buttonhole. She also embellished the pieces with obsidian star beads, glass beads, thread purl, and hand-dyed fabrics hand-cut into leaves. In 1999 Susan was interested in selling her work at Nantucket Looms, and because Liz, then the owner, made her feel loved, there was nowhere else she wanted to feature her work. To Susan's great relief, she said that Liz accepted the pieces, priced them accordingly, then said, "Let's see what happens." Soon afterwards Liz called to announce, "They all sold! Do you have any more?" Beginning in 2020 Susan has embraced new art forms of watercolor, gouache, and pen and ink to illustrate the lives of remarkable Nantucket women through her whimsical paintings. In doing so, she herself has become one of the island's most notable and remarkable women.

LEFT: In the den, the shelves are styled with books collected on Nantucket, which are bookended by carpet balls. At the bottom is Michael Bacle's white whale wood hand-carving named *Moby Dick*. Cypress-lined walls feature an embroidered narrative titled *Eliza Spencer Brock (1810-99)*, stitched by Susan Boardman, and an oil painting by Elle Foley.

In the tranquil entryway foyer, a grouping of Nantucket lightship baskets and handcrafted finials are displayed on the antique walnut drop-leaf table with an arrangement of hydrangeas and wildflowers from the garden. Above, hangs a display of framed handwoven tapestries by Nantucket Looms Master Weaver, Rebecca Jusko Peraner, two of which are crafted to incorporate the owner's personal collections of ivory alphabet letters. These letters were used in the early nineteenth century

REBECCA JUSKO PERANER
MASTER WEAVER

Rebecca Jusko Peraner, a graduate of Rhode Island School of Design who came to Nantucket as an apprentice to Andrew Oates, today is a master weaver and partner of Nantucket Looms. Her craft has included handwoven tapestries since 1998. These tapestries incorporate the weaving of found objects into one-of-a-kind heirloom vignettes that complement a range of interior design styles, creating what she describes as "a little bit of heart and soul." Growing up in Connecticut in a house surrounded with family collections of everything from woven baskets to old English ironware, Rebecca subliminally embraced her family's love of collections along with an appreciation for authentic handwoven textiles. The inspiration for her tapestry design was found in the numerous shells she gathered on many long walks along the Nantucket beaches with her mother and two daughters. Reimagining the weaving patterns she uses in the Nantucket Looms weaving studio, Rebecca began to embellish her weaving with sea life—scallop shells, sand dollars, and starfish—creating fanciful vignettes, woven with linen and hand-dyed yarn, by raising and lowering the warp threads on the loom. The flat objects are literally locked into place as the shuttle passes back and forth across the warp. She immensely enjoys the evolution of each project from collecting and preparing the objects to the time-consuming process of preparing the loom to final completion. As the idea for the tapestries blossomed, she began incorporating eclectic collectibles and pieces with personal meaning, such as watch parts, fishing lures, antique ivory alphabet pieces, stamps, and even seed pods, into handwoven works of art. Each piece is framed for display. Working in collaboration with the Nantucket Looms clients, Rebecca creates specialty tapestries upon request, such as heart-shaped beach rocks gathered by a husband for his wife, sharing the joy of her craft with those who wish to incorporate sentiment into their decor.

to teach children to read and write. The beautiful rug, handwoven in soothing pastel tones by Nantucket Looms artisan Hillary Anapol, is a lovely contrast to the reclaimed oak wood floors used throughout the house. Linen yarn in natural earthy hues was selected to complement the objets d'art.

In a hallway nearby on the antique spindle leg table is a stack of Mark Sutherland's bone ditty boxes inspired by the nearby display of nineteenth-century wooden Shaker boxes. These oval boxes were originally used to store herbs, spices, and sewing notions. This vignette is balanced by a contemporary lithograph by Christopher Brown, a vintage stool with modern upholstery, and a woven basket by Nina Webb.

Towards the back of the home, the library walls are paneled in three-hundred-year-old Midnight Heart Cypress Wood, sourced from a Georgia bog. It provides a luxurious backdrop for the wall art that features an embroidered narrative by Susan Boardman and a painting of South Wharf by Elle Foley. The bookshelves showcase a collection of books purchased on Nantucket, carpet balls, and Michael Bacle's wood hand-carving of a white whale named *Moby Dick*.

A screened porch serves as an extension of the home where the owner spends leisurely afternoons and holds large family gatherings. A vintage "Children At Play" sign is a nod to these special times. Beyond the kitchen lies a lush garden courtyard designed by the owner in collaboration with local landscaper Lindsay Mohr and woodworker Todd Stout. The espaliered tree is a flowering crab apple. Nestled in a bed of lavender is a terra-cotta pot filled with an assortment of herbs, rudbeckia, and chocolate cosmos. A pathway of stepping stones lined with calamintha leads to the garden gate adding to the abundant magic of Cachalot.

OPPOSITE: In the entry foyer is a wool rug handwoven by artisan Hillary Anapol. Hillary worked with the owner on the color selection and the pattern of weave. Above the drop leaf walnut table is a grouping of tapestries handwoven by Nantucket Looms Master Weaver Rebecca Jusko Peraner that feature shells, sand dollars, and ivory alphabet pieces collected by the owner. Displayed on the table are lightship baskets and finials in the shape of artichokes and pineapples. These pieces were hand carved by Eric Bogdahn and painted by Noelle Walters. The two antique chairs flanking the table have been upholstered in Rogers and Goffigon's Cervo linen and chenille velvet fabric.

ABOVE: A round table and chairs are the centerpiece of the courtyard garden. A shingled garden house covered with roses supported by latticework is surrounded by a medley of potted plants, topiaries, and boxwood bushes. **OPPOSITE**: A pathway of stepping stones lined with calamintha and ilex shrubs, excellent choices for a border, leads to the garden gate.

LYDIA

◆

A Charming Wharf
Cottage

Summer living is easy at Lydia, a snug cottage perched on the Easy Street Basin waterfront on Nantucket's Old North Wharf—just steps away from the harborside town. "Cottages are the best thing . . . funky . . . charming . . . sweep the sand from the front door right out the back door," said Liz Winship. The one-bedroom, one-bath charmer with an addition, or wart, to use island vernacular, is hugged by a pocket-size garden and deck that extends the living space in the summertime. The Lydia ambience is on point: Take in the pretty view of Nantucket's skyline, feel the wharf vibe, the salty breezes and, from a ring-side seat at the golden hour, watch the moon begin its ascent over Nantucket Sound. Named after the whaling ship Lydia, which was owned by Henry and Charles Coffin, the 343-square-foot former fish shanty is one of many similar structures built on the wharf in the 1870s to replace the original structures destroyed by the Great Fire of 1846. In the early twentieth century the tiny shacks were converted into artist studios, summer cottages, and picnic houses.

The Old North Wharf is one of five wharves plus a town pier on Nantucket's harbor front and is the only one that is residential and privately owned by individual families. The stone foundation is visible at low tide. A stone's throw from Lydia is the meeting house of the Wharf Rat Club, which was established in 1927 and was officially named in 1971 for the Grateful Dead song "Wharf Rat," written by Jerry Garcia. Fishermen, sailors, and Nantucket natives first gathered there around a potbellied stove in what was then a fishing supply store to have a gam, the Nantucket term for a get-together, to swap stories and hang out. There are no membership fees, no

PREVIOUS PAGES: Lydia, one of the charming wharf cottages on Old North Wharf, is known as an idyllic space to host family and friends. It is noticeable due to its powder blue door, quaint stature, and sizable lawn overlooking Nantucket Harbor. To make the most of the space, several seating areas have been created in the cozy cottage. Natural-fiber rugs cover the splatter-painted floor. A weathered pine console table serves as a space for enjoying meals and offers storage and a place to display collections. **RIGHT:** The one-room charmer is hugged by a garden and a picket fence lined with flowering hydrangea plants. A deck extends the living space in time of warmer weather.

PREVIOUS PAGES: With a view across the harbor, a Malawi cane barrel chair and a sofa covered in a linen pinstripe fabric brings comfort to the seating area. Denim Belgian linen fringe pillows are paired with a mandala-inspired hand-blocked linen lumbar pillow and a handwoven cashmere throw in dune, adding layers of texture and color to the space. The original awning windows open out to let the sea breeze in. OPPOSITE: A classic striped well-worn Nantucket Looms cotton boatneck sweater and indigo apron hang from a nearby door. On the rustic coffee table is a porcelain dory boat model, and in the background on the wall is a Robert Stark Jr. *Red Sail* oil painting, for which he is famous. ABOVE: A teak bowl filled with a collection of antique glove stretchers, a vintage Cloth Company comb scrimshawed with a Nantucket quarterboard, and old clothespins are displayed on the coffee table.

ABOVE: On top of the storage console, a bird decoy gazes towards a green ship's prism light, used to disperse light on the decks of a boat, adding a colorful bit of charm to a collection of books that includes a facsimile of *Anni Albers Notebook 1970–1980*. Albers was Andy Oates's weaving instructor at Black Mountain College in North Carolina. OPPOSITE: A petite bouclé barrel chair features a handwoven navy-and-ivory-striped cotton throw with a linen accent pillow. Maritime details include an original whaling ship painting, a bird decoy by Mark McNair, and a nautical rope retrieving pole.

OPPOSITE: Displayed on a set of built-in shelves in the shiplike galley kitchen are three miniature handwoven lightship baskets, along with a collection of vintage glass bottles, kitchen tools, marmalade and caviar jars, and a clotted cream container. ABOVE: A charming cottage corner is enhanced with the tapestry of sand-dollar shells, handwoven by Rebecca Jusko Peraner, and a photograph taken by Andy Oates.

regular meetings, and no rules. The only requirement for entry is to have the ability to tell a good story. The management operates in a shroud of mystery, adding allure to club membership. Some people have waited twenty years to become a member, and others never made it.

Nantucket Looms brings cottage charm to Lydia. The port of entry to the pitched roof rectangular structure is a welcoming haint blue—a blend of sea and sky. The latch windows and picket fence add a touch of authenticity. The paint-splattered floor is a fine example of early 1900s Yankee ingenuity and an idea borrowed from classic enamelware. Old worn floors were painted with leftover paint and then splattered to make them decorative. Near the door are vintage Nantucket Looms pieces—a tote bag and CPO (chief petty officer) jacket, which should always be kept within reach as an extra layer for warmth or as a Nantucket-style unisex dinner jacket, and an American flag embellished with scallop shells by Nantucket Looms Master Weaver Rebecca Jusko Peraner. The ship's galley-style kitchen showcases early

LIA MARKS
TAILOR

From the moment Andy Oates and Bill Euler met Lia Marks in 1968, they knew she would become an important member of their Nantucket Looms family. An accomplished seamstress from Germany, Lia was initially commissioned to make men's neckties and women's skirts for the shop, which was a way to showcase the handwoven textiles made in the weaving studio. Lia then suggested they use Nantucket Looms handwoven tweeds to make men's and women's jackets inspired by the classic shirt jacket often worn by chief petty officers in the US Navy. On an island of sailors, Lia's jackets were an instant success, and the Nantucket CPO was born. Often layered with a boat-neck sweater and button-down, the CPO is a jacket for all seasons, and Nantucket's answer to the sports coat. It is estimated that Lia made close to 10,000 jackets over the course of five decades. It was a special experience going into Nantucket Looms where Liz would measure you for a jacket, and you could select from a variety of tweeds to pair with a number of colorful Liberty of London cotton linings. No jacket was ever the same. Lia Marks passed away on November 13, 2022, a month after celebrating her ninety-seventh birthday. Today, Nantucket Looms has launched the CPO 2.0, which is constructed with Lia's same patterns for a new generation of Nantucketers.

island curiosities, including a pennant and old Nantucket Wharf Rat Club mug. Preparations are underway for a sandwich lunch on the wharf. A ship's light hanging from the ceiling adds to the nautical flavor of the cottage.

In the living room, a Malawi barrel cane chair and a sofa covered in a linen pinstripe fabric bring comfort to the seating area. Denim Belgian linen fringe pillows are paired with a mandala-inspired, hand-blocked linen lumbar pillow and a handwoven cashmere throw in a dune hue, adding layers of texture and color to the space. A Robert Stark Jr. highly sought-after *Red Sail* painting hangs on the corner wall. Stark painted his solitary-dory-with-red-sail theme paintings for forty years. Stark's studio and gallery used to be on the Old North Wharf, and one can imagine him painting this just steps away from Lydia. The original awning windows are a special feature. They can be open even when it's raining to let in fresh air. The floor is covered with a custom handwoven sisal rug. On the coffee table is a rustic teak bowl filled with antique glove spreaders that were used to restore the shape of leather gloves, a comb in the shape of a fish stamped with a Nantucket quarterboard lettering from the Cloth Company days, and old clothespins. The dory model echoes the elements of the Stark painting. A classic striped well-worn Nantucket Looms cotton sweater and indigo apron complete the nautical look. These are the components of Nantucket Looms cottage style. A John Austin painting (not seen in photograph) that evokes the Bear Street house is included in a display over a console, a new piece made to look old. A ship's deck prism light, used to disperse light on the decks of a boat, adds a colorful bit of charm to a collection of books that includes a facsimile of *Anni Albers Notebook 1970–1980.*

In the addition, next to the deck, a modern chair sits beneath the haint blue-painted ceiling that can be flipped down to batten the hatches in stormy weather. The soft white-hued wall paint color was specially chosen to reflect the light and changing colors of the water and sky throughout the day. The indoor-outdoor teak stools with woven seat covers complement the weathered-pine console that serves as a table top for snacks and refreshments and also provides additional storage. Dining can be enjoyed on the adjacent deck with a front-row seat where one can relish watching the bustle of harbor life. There's no better way to spend a lazy summer afternoon than sitting in a deck chair on the dock with a favorite read.

PREVIOUS PAGE: The paint-splattered floor is a fine example of early 1900s Yankee ingenuity and an idea borrowed from classic enamelware. Old worn floors were painted with leftover paint and then splattered to make them decorative. A rustic ladder leads to a storage loft. The Dutch door is styled with an American flag tapestry by Rebecca Jusko Peraner and everyday essentials, including a basket filled with beach towels, a CPO jacket tailored by Lia Marks, and tote bags. The ship galley-style kitchen showcases early island curiosities, including a pennant and old Nantucket Wharf Rat Club mug. OPPOSITE AND ABOVE: Outdoor dining can be enjoyed on the adjacent deck while watching the bustle of harbor life.

FEATHER'S NEST

✦

A Historic House
in Town

The Nantucket Looms style can be incorporated in houses of all ages and sizes, from pool-house cabañas to historic homes. This two-story Nantucket house, named Feather's Nest, was built in 1794 near the center of town on a street covered with sand and lined with houses where, through open windows, one could feel the breezes and listen to the pass, meaning eavesdrop.

Over two hundred years later, what seemed to be a good idea turned into a wonderful opportunity. A desire for more driveway space led to the purchase of Feather's Nest, which was at the time the house next door to the owner's primary residence. His original intention was to throw a coat of paint on the old house, rent it, and use the convenience of the driveway.

But as the owner became aware of the beauty of the old house, he reversed course, choosing instead to preserve it and move in himself. A local firm, Main Street Construction, was contracted to assist the Nantucket Looms design team in bringing the old house back to life by preserving the original details—the heart pine floors, the previously covered-up old exposed beams, the unique stairway—and by repurposing the special attic space into a secluded hideaway. When this work was completed, the owner loved the house so much he immediately moved in.

In consideration of the aesthetic and design of the house, along with the homeowner's preferences for antiques, folk art, collections of interesting things, and added touches of whimsy, the vision for Feather's Nest included incorporating the natural color palette of Nantucket into the home as a connection to the island. "We will always find ways to incorporate meaningful collections, so your home is a reflection of what you love," said Stephanie Hall, Nantucket Looms principal designer. "We mix the old with the new and are always on the lookout for curiosities and pieces with interesting stories."

A neutral palette was used throughout Feather's Nest, with the exception of the dining room, to accentuate architectural details. In the living room emphasis is given to an exposed corner beam, heart pine floors, and a collection of tramp art, a form of art popular ca. 1870 to 1940 that was created by hobos who whittled wooden cigar boxes into interesting objects. An assemblage of furnishings—a formal velvet Chesterfield sofa, a leather chair trimmed with nailheads, and a pair of chairs covered in a textured fabric, along more modern pieces—combine to create a masculine aesthetic. The antique bronze mirror with exaggerated rivets complements the leather chair with metal accents. In the spirit of a Nantucket Looms home, organic pieces such as the jute rug and the sculptural shape of the root coffee table are brought in to balance the more sophisticated elements.

The rich high-gloss hue on the walls of the dining room creates the feel of an old-world whaling captain's formal stateroom, where he entertained in the evenings. A one-of-a-kind rug, woven in India, was chosen to dress the room.

In the family-size kitchen the original fireplace is enhanced with a mantel constructed with a beam found in the attic. A "Just Ahead" boatyard sign sends a warning signal near a butler staircase that gives access to the second floor. The sign is an example of colorful and sometimes humorous vintage signage commonly found in the shop. A rug is intentionally absent due to this being a high-traffic area.

PAGE 173: A jewel-box effect is achieved by painting the house's dining room walls, ceiling, and trim all in the same color of a rich high-gloss shade of blue. Italian creamware apothecary jars, set on either side of a mixed-media piece by David Wiggins, adorn the mantel. **ABOVE**: A layered tabletop look is achieved by using a variety of ceramic plates and bowls presented on a seagrass charger with a Nantucket Looms cotton napkin. **OPPOSITE**: A closet that was transformed into a bar is situated in a niche between the living and dining rooms. Painted in the same color as the dining room, it is embellished in the back and on the sides with a Peter Fasano printed grasscloth for texture.

The adjacent family room leads out of doors and is the most contemporary space in the house. Exposed ceiling beams, a large wooden whale carving crafted by Michael Bacle, and a rustic pine coffee table complement the hues of the painting by Nantucket artist Joan Albaugh, whose images of houses are always painted without windows. The second-floor bedrooms are quiet spaces where one can escape from the rest of the house and where luxurious amenities abound. The art of bed making at Nantucket Looms consists of luxurious linens woven in Italy from 100-percent long-staple cotton, including crisp bright white cotton sheets and a coverlet topped with a comforter encased in a duvet. Finishing touches include decorative pillows, and there's always a soft handwoven throw to wrap up in. Make sure to have a tray with everything you need at nighttime within close

DAVID WIGGINS
MIXED-MEDIA ARTIST

David Wiggins was already a highly regarded, accomplished painter—best known for his magnificent frescoes painted in the Americana folk art style—when he moved to Nantucket in the early 1990s. Soon afterwards he was invited by Liz Winship to collaborate with fellow artist Kevin Paulson, in an art show at Nantucket Looms. "David Wiggins is a hugely talented artist with his own stylistic approach and is definitely one of the best," Liz said. "He really pushes the envelope." Originally from a family of art and antiques dealers in New Hampshire, David studied art in Florence, Italy, and on the Greek island of Poros where he was exposed to vivid bold colors and unique perspectives of light. After returning home from his travels, he took ownership of the family business, Wiggins Brothers Antiques, where he honed his expertise and knowledge as a period decorator. David has a rare versatility—and generates excitement in whatever style he works in—early and mid-century modernism, Americana folk art, or abstract expressionism. For David, the process of painting is an adventure in the use of mixed media: tar, plaster, oil paints, glazes, paper, cardboard, sand. He mostly uses the floor as his easel to control the fluid paints he prefers to use. David finds satisfaction embracing the dual challenges of bringing traditional styles into the next generation and in self-expression—endeavoring to reveal what comes to him from a metaphysical inner sense, never quite knowing what the focus of a painting will be until a culminating idea comes to him, which mostly happens at end of the process.

PREVIOUS PAGES: In the living room, emphasis is given to an exposed corner beam, heart pine floors, a French bronze rivet mirror, and a collection of tramp art—a popular form of folk art from ca. 1870 to 1940—to the right of the window. Organic elements include a root coffee table, rope-wrapped light fixture, a French harvest basket, and the natural jute rug that anchors the space. An assemblage of furnishings—a formal velvet Chesterfield sofa, a leather chair trimmed with nailheads, and a pair of chairs covered in a textured fabric, along with contemporary pieces—combine to create a masculine aesthetic. RIGHT: Tucked at the end of the hallway, a study has been created by adding bookshelves and cabinets with leather door pulls. Displayed on the shelves is a piece of tramp art. A photograph by Ben Larrabee hangs on a nearby wall.

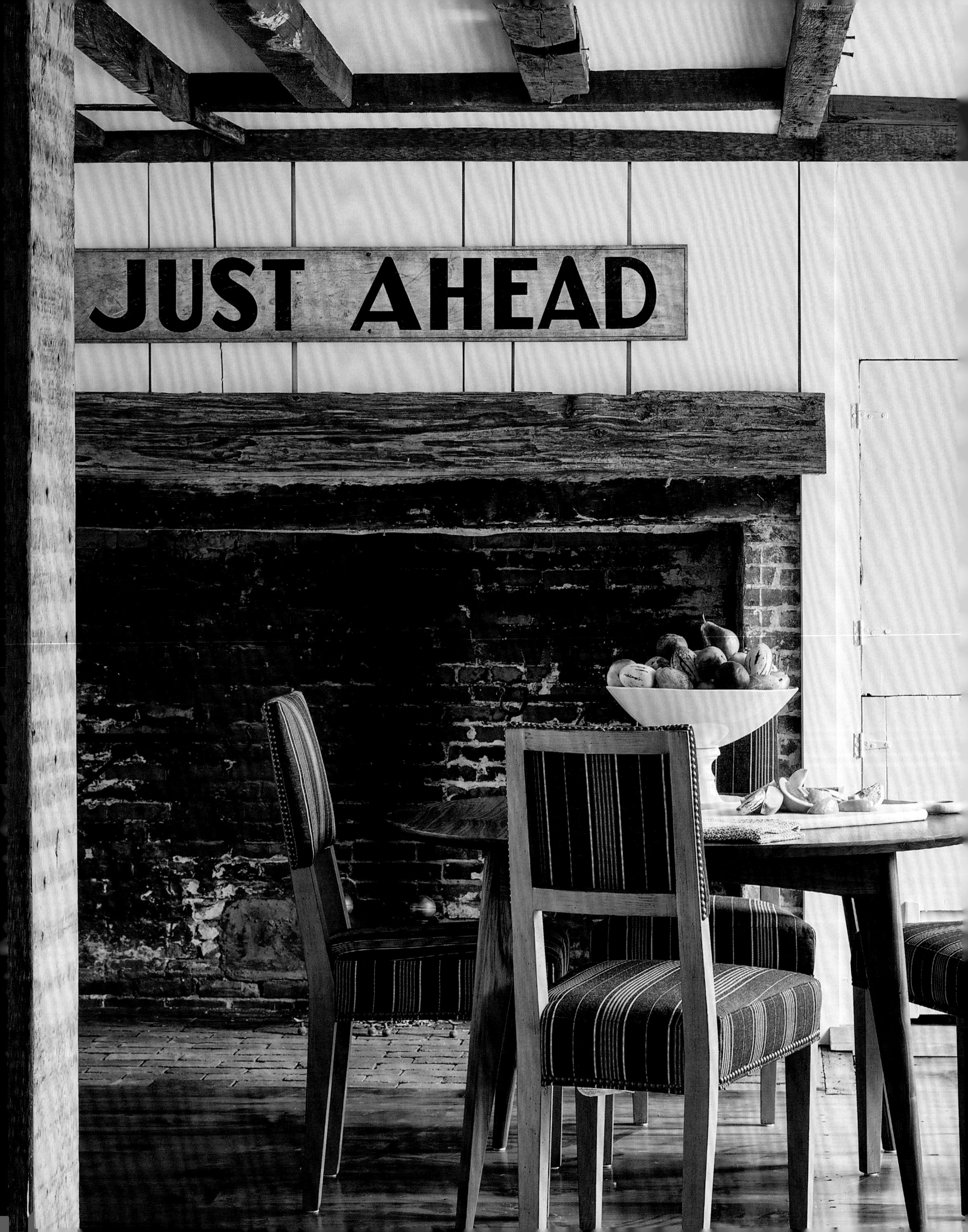
JUST AHEAD

LEFT: The family-size kitchen includes a breakfast table with four upholstered chairs in a Perennials fabric with nailhead trim. A vintage map of Nantucket hangs in the butler's staircase. The original fireplace is enhanced with a mantel constructed with a beam found in the attic. A vintage "Just Ahead" boatyard sign is playfully displayed above it. **FOLLOWING PAGES:** In the living room, the nautical theme of the home can be seen in the buoy side lamps, the large whale carving crafted by Michael Bacle, and the shades of blue in the fabrics. A Joan Albaugh painting of her popular windowless house is on display. A cast resin planter holds a fern.

reach—a carafe for water, a trinket box to hold jewelry, and a favorite book.

As you climb the steep set of stairs to the attic using the nautical rope handrail, you get the feeling of being aboard a ship because of the high-pitched shiplap ceilings and the built-in bunk beds. If you look closely at one of the original exposed wooden beams, you will see the hand-carved inscription by the carpenter from the year 1822. Wall-to-wall carpeting adds warmth, and the varying shades of blue invoke the feeling of being at sea. Contemporary American fabrics are rooted in nautical themes. The widow's walk with a view of Nantucket Harbor is accessed by a spiral staircase through a ceiling hatch. You can imagine what it was like to be on this widow's walk in the 1800s watching for the return of a ship after a five-year voyage at sea.

MICHAEL AND SUSAN BACLE
CARVERS

For Michael Bacle, one thing leads to another. Liz Winship remembers the first time he walked into Nantucket Looms carrying one of his pieces of Americana folk art—a hand-carved swan—by the neck. Michael, who has studied carving and painting under Mark McNair, a modern master of bird carving, found inspiration in the arts and crafts scene on the island and wanted to be a part of it. After a slow start with duck decoys, Michael found success when he switched to carving sculptures of swans, a Nantucket waterbird; people on the island find their primitive renditions irresistible. Beside the fact he enjoys carving shapes of these majestic creatures, when he heard an auctioneer comment he could never get enough large hand-carved wood whales—Michael began carving what he describes as an abstract whale, or a folk-art style impression of a whale, in two-, three-, and seven-foot lengths for Nantucket Looms. Michael sources cypress and juniper for his sculptures from the Carolinas. Once the design of the sculpture is established, he uses a bandsaw to carve the shape of the object in wood, then follows with a wood rasp and chisel to refine and smooth the sculpture. The swans and whales are finished with six to seven coats of milk paint, off-white (for Moby Dick replicas), or black by his wife, Susan Bacle, an accomplished artist in her own right who carves and paints shore birds and schools of fish, which are mounted on driftwood for display. Susan and Michael Bacle's primitive Americana folk art is timeless and adorns the walls and mantels of houses big and small, from the shores of Nantucket and beyond.

OPPOSITE AND ABOVE: In the attic rooms, the high-pitched shiplap ceiling and built-in bunk beds maximize the space under the eaves. Wall-to-wall carpeting adds warmth and sound proofing to the floors below. Contemporary American fabrics in varying shades of blue are rooted in nautical themes. To the left, on the wall above the white chair, is a photograph of a dock by Lauren Jacobson Marttila, and next to the bunk beds is a photograph of a sailboat by Ben Larrabee.

RIGHT: In the guest room are a queen-size cane bed and painted grasscloth side tables. Prints of feathers are a nod to the name of the house. The art of Nantucket Looms bed making consists of luxurious, crisp bright white linens woven in Italy from 100-percent long-staple cotton and a coverlet topped with a comforter encased in a duvet. Finishing touches include decorative pillows, and there's always a soft handwoven throw to wrap up in.

SETH COFFIN HOUSE

A Captain's Quarters

Nantucket Looms style brings a sense of occasion with its elegant, well-appointed interior design in honoring the history of this quintessential nineteenth-century ship captain's house. It was once considered the epitome of formal living on a quiet shady roadway festooned with a collection of sheltering trees—elm, silver maple, white ash—and an exquisite honey locust specimen. The house is described by its owner—a third generation Nantucketer—as "a very cool period house with the help of Nantucket Looms interior design team." It is located in the Fish Lots near the harbor, just a stone's throw from cobblestoned Main Street and within earshot of the melodious sound of ringing church bells at the Second Congressional Meeting House Society. The Fish Lots, one of the town's earliest neighborhoods, was established in 1717 by the Proprietors and named for the codfish dried on wooden racks by local fishermen. The shipshape formality of this captain's house reveals an American sensibility in Nantucket Looms artful blending of traditional elements with sophisticated details, pairing family heirlooms with contemporary pieces, all of which coalesce to tell a modern-day family story.

This classic two-story house was built from 1832 to 1834 by whaling ship captain Seth Coffin Jr. in the fashionable Greek Revival style of the day, a period aesthetic that seeped into the island's architectural design with the decline of the Quaker era. The owners prize the eight fireplaces, five bedrooms, and exceptionally large rooms with high ceilings

The Seth Coffin House was once an upholstery shop and ladies dress shop, eventually becoming Nantucket's Center for Elder Affairs. Today, it is once again a beloved family home. Updating a period look with fresh and

PREVIOUS PAGES: Nantucket-style fanback Windsor chairs surround an oval table in the dining room of this nineteenth-century ship captain's house. Pictured in the background is one of the eight original fireplaces in the house. RIGHT: A family collection of Mottahedeh Blue Canton pottery. Nantucket whaling captains often brought home treasures such as this from their travels around the globe.

ABOVE: An oil painting by American artist Stanley Grant Middleton is displayed on the wall above an antique demilune cabinet that is near a corner in the dining room. **OPPOSITE**: Handcrafted cabinetry shelves display the homeowner's family heirlooms, including Canton pottery, a ship model, and sailing trophies, along with contemporary paintings. **FOLLOWING PAGES**: On the far left, family silhouettes can be seen on the living room wall. On the right in a sitting room is a painting by Joan Albaugh incorporating the play of light and shadow—a feature of her moody studies of Nantucket off-season that often include windowless houses.

modern appeal involves studious attention to detail. The light-filled entry hall introduces the soft-hued palette of whites, creams, and shades of green and blue in sharp contrast to the rich high gloss of the dark wood banister and historic yellow pine floors. Look closely and you can see the ivory mortgage button, a proud Nantucket tradition that symbolizes the property is owned free and clear, the mortgage has been paid in full, and no liens exist against the property. Child silhouette portraits, watercolors, oils, and photographs mix beautifully together. Handcrafted cabinetry proudly displays the homeowner's family heirlooms, such as the Canton pottery, a ship model alongside contemporary paintings, and sailing trophies.

This gracious ship captain's house is a wish fulfilled as it encapsulates all the traditional elements of house architecture one looks for while walking the storied streets of Nantucket Island—a formal, classic period residence filled with the beauty, lightness, and energy of island life today. The seaside charm and modernity of this historical house is a beautiful representation of Nantucket Looms style.

JOAN ALBAUGH
ARTIST

Since the 1990s Joan Albaugh has been a good friend of Nantucket Looms. "I owe a lot of my success as an island artist to having found a home at the Looms thirty years ago," she said. Joan moved to Nantucket with an artist's dream to create a life for herself on the island. After exhibiting and making her first sale at the Artists Association of Nantucket, she was encouraged by the buyer of that painting to approach Liz Winship at Nantucket Looms. Liz knew that people would be drawn to Joan's strong color palettes and isolated themes and felt she would find great success at Nantucket Looms. Invigorated by the play of light and shadow on objects in Nantucket's off-season—an isolated house, an empty pool, a buoy, or a bush—Joan brings her brush to the canvas to create contemplative works featuring windowless houses, landscapes, and water. Her contemporary and meditative works of art bring their own quiet beauty to many island homes. A graduate of the School of the Museum of Fine Arts, Boston, Joan also received a BFA from Tufts University in 1981. Joan exhibited in 2022 at the Arctic Circle Residency, Svalbard, Norway, and most recently was the recipient of the People's Choice Award, Artists Association of Nantucket, in 2019.

OPPOSITE. The entry introduces the home's soft-hued palette of whites, creams, and shades of green and blue, which are in sharp contrast to the rich high gloss of the dark wood banister and historic yellow-pine floors. On the newel post is an ivory mortgage button, a proud Nantucket tradition symbolizing that the mortgage has been paid in full and no liens exist against the property. **ABOVE**: Displayed in the front hall is an 1853 print titled *Clipper Ship "Sweepstakes,"* which is inscribed "To Aaron J. Westervelt, Esq. builder of the New York—This print is respectfully dedicated by the Publishers." It is befittingly framed in an elaborative bonnet-top pediment.

BEACH BUCKET

A Summer
Retreat

This classic charmer, located in the neighborhood known as the Cliff, captures the imagination making it the perfect summer retreat. The house was built in 1930, the same year the Whaling Museum opened to the public in the Hadwen & Barney Oil and Candle Factory in nearby downtown Nantucket. The architecture of the house is typical of the seventeenth-century lean-to style, a two-story shingled structure distinguished by a steeply sloping roof with an expanded dormer that allows space for additional light and a third-story garret. A widow's walk atop the roof has wonderful views of Nantucket Sound and a charming cobblestone alley below. In the garden, roses and large blooms of hydrangeas in vibrant shades of purples and blues are enclosed by a white picket fence capped with a ship's rail, imparting a picturesque island ambiance along with a nod to the whaling era.

Dressed in the colors of summer with lighter blues, pastels, and bright whites, the decor has the feeling of a proper historic coastal home. Beautiful linens and handwoven textiles add a refined sophistication. The front entry flows into the living room, the largest room in the house, with a traditional staircase. Multiple arrangements of furnishings are centered around the fireplace. Two skirted swivel chairs upholstered in a dusty blue ikat fabric accompany a woven linen sofa by Lee Industries featuring a bench seat cushion. Brooke Gherardini, a Nantucket Looms interior designer said, "One of my favorite features of this room is the handwoven wool and silk custom cut-to-fit rug with braided rope detailing. Its large scale grounds the space while lending a quiet elegance to the overall design." In a far corner of the living

PREVIOUS PAGES: The painting, *Madaket Harbor*, by Nantucket artist Jocelyn Sandor Urban makes a bold statement on this enclosed porch. Two deep-barrel chairs constructed of abaca rope and Danish cording provide comfortable seating. Instead of a traditional coffee table, a trio of tables is artfully arranged in front of the sofa. **LEFT:** In a far corner of the living room is a window seat with a tufted cushion and an assortment of colorful patterned pillows. Books, a ceramic dish, and a small oil painting, *Windswept Bogs*, by M.J. Levy Dickson are elegantly displayed on the coffee table in a teal faux shagreen tray next to a reactive glaze ceramic pot filled with blooming hydrangea flowers.

FOLLOWING PAGES: A wool rug dresses the dining room. The chairs surrounding the custom hand-painted dining room table are upholstered in C&C Milano silk and wool-blended fabric and a Holland & Sherry woven blue geometric linen fabric, grounded with a natural nailhead detail. An abstract painting, *The Kerosene House*, by M.J. Levy Dickson hangs above the cream-colored buffet. It adds dramatic bursts of blue and greens to the room. The buffet holds a collection of antique mochaware and ironware.

room is a window seat with a tufted cushion and an assortment of colorful patterned pillows

In the dining room, a rug designed by Nantucket Looms covers the floor where the furniture is arranged so guests can appreciate the stunning artwork and understated beauty of the Phillip Jeffries grasscloth wallpaper. The chairs surrounding the contemporary table are upholstered in a sea glass and gray-hued fabric, complementing the Elizabeth Eakins linen fabric draperies. An abstract painting by M.J. Levy Dickson hangs above the buffet adding saturated bursts of blue and green to the room. The buffet holds a collection of antique mochaware and ironware. These types of earthenware pottery were a favorite of Bill, Andy, and Liz, who displayed their collections as pieces of art.

Comfort is at its finest on the enclosed porch. Shingled walls, which are original to the house, were painted white to enhance their texture, and the low ceiling, layered with bead board, was brushed with a high-gloss

M.J. LEVY DICKSON
PAINTER

The dynamic artistry of M.J. Levy Dickson is inspired by the beauty she experiences every day on Nantucket. "M.J.'s abstract interpretation of nature in her works allows the viewer to see the world in an entirely different way," said Bess Clarke. "We have been fortunate to represent M.J. over the years and showcase the variety of her art." M.J.'s creativity is the art of the possible, the fusion of harmonious elements with variations of light and shadow, colorful accents, and shapes revealed in interesting and thought-provoking ways. A self-described visual thinker, M.J. said, "What I love is color. Any vehicle I can use is appealing to me. I've enjoyed making the sky green and the landscape blue. Just because you haven't seen it doesn't mean it doesn't exist." Her rich body of work includes drawings, paintings, sculpture, installation work, printmaking, and even fabrication of hand-molded sea glass. M.J. has taught at Massachusetts Institute of Technology, Boston Architectural College, and Wenzhou-Kean University in Wenzhou, China, and served as artist-in-residence at the Perkins School for the Blind in Watertown, Massachusetts, where she expanded on her theories for making art accessible to populations that perceive it in different ways. If there's one person in the world who can light up a child's life with the joy of artistic expression, it's M.J. Levy Dickson.

white. A workspace is outfitted with a specially crafted table for playing games and doing puzzles, which also serves double duty as extra space for entertaining. The room is furnished with a skirted sofa, upholstered in linen and layered with patterned pillows, a cushioned bench, and two woven swivel chairs. A trio of side tables provides surfaces to hold a drink, a book, or a pretty plant, and they are petite enough to be shifted around the space. Displayed on a side table is a one-of-a-kind model of the 1870s sloop yacht *Vigilant*, hand-carved by marine artisan Mark Sutherland. The beauty of a summery moment continues on the flower-laden deck.

MARK SUTHERLAND
MODEL-BOAT MAKER

For Mark Sutherland, a self-described marine artisan, his career took off in 1981 when he received a call from Bill Euler, co-owner of Nantucket Looms, asking him to carve a dory model for the shop. Not only did Euler and his partner Andy Oates begin to buy Sutherland's boats for the shop, but they began their own collection, too. That was the beginning of the dories, and soon Sutherland's repertoire included sailing dories, skiffs, Marshall catboats, ship replicas, and colorful Beetle Cats, the famed racing craft of Nantucket's Rainbow Fleet and "the quintessential Nantucket boat, after the whale boat," wrote Michael Harrison of the Nantucket Historical Association. Nantucketers still marvel today over Sutherland's whalebone carvings of Beetle boats in a chase. Today it is illegal to carve whalebone, or sell it in the US, unless it was procured before 1973. Sutherland's half-hull ships were sold exclusively at Nantucket Looms, as well as his whalebone ditty boxes like those once used by sailors to collect odds and ends. Since those early days Sutherland has been commissioned to build hundreds of boat models in all shapes and sizes. Many are collectibles, and some are museum pieces. Sutherland also builds full-size vessels that sail the open sea. Sutherland now specializes in models of nineteenth- and twentieth-century ships and was commissioned by the Nantucket Historical Association to build a rigged model of the Nantucket whaleship—the Essex—for a display at the Whaling Museum to coincide with the publication of Nathaniel Philbrick's book, *Heart of the Sea*, the true story of Herman Melville's fictitious Moby Dick. Sutherland returns to Nantucket every summer and teaches "How to carve and race a small pond boat" at the Nantucket Historical Association's 1800 House where, as he said, "The dories live on."

OPPOSITE, CLOCKWISE FROM TOP LEFT: The dining table is set with off-white glazed stone dinnerware, wine glasses, and tapered brass candlesticks with small arrangements of Queen Anne's lace to add a touch of simple beauty. These draperies are a custom cotton-and-linen blend and are finished with a Romo fabric tape border. An abstract interpretation of nature by M.J. Levy Dickson lights up the space above the console in the dining room. An upholstered ottoman with a nailhead finish is covered with a Nantucket Looms handwoven ivory mohair-and-silk throw. ABOVE: Mark Sutherland's handcrafted ship model is a recreation of an 1870s sloop yacht. These yachts were known as "skimming dishes" as they were wide and had a shallow draft centerboard and a combination of sails.

OPPOSITE AND ABOVE: The beauty of a summer moment takes place on the flower-laden deck, located just a few steps from the garden. Contemporary teak furniture provides a relaxing environment for entertaining.

Brunch in the Garden at Mitchell House

Nantucket's Upper Main Street is one of the most beautiful streets in America. The pristine stately houses built by the great merchants of the whaling era from the early eighteenth century until the mid-nineteenth century are a vision to behold. Even today, there's always something new to see. But one must know what to look for.

One house worth taking a closer look at is the grand white clapboard Colonial on Main Street, a National Historic Landmark that has occupied this corner of Nantucket's historic downtown district since 1799. The house has experienced many reincarnations throughout its long history as the home of several of Nantucket's wealthiest whaling merchants. While the rear portion of

the house dates from the early 1700s, the main house was built between 1794 and 1797 in what is now the Nantucket Historic District. At one time the structure was divided to create a duplex to accommodate two families, and outbuildings on the one-and-a-half–acre property included a wagon shed, a boarding stable for horses, and a candle factory for processing whale oil into the candles preferred by Thomas Jefferson.

Today, a broad expanse of magnificent lawn edged with kousa dogwood, honey locust, and Leonard Messel magnolia trees spreads from the covered back porch of the house to the edge of a hidden Eden designed by Laura Davison of Sean O'Callaghan Landscaping, a Nantucket firm. Laura transformed what was once a big sunken

area into what she describes as a "moon garden," a private sequestered shady area of delicate sweetness for sitting and visiting filled with white flowers and variegated leaves. Steps descend into a small formal bosquet-style garden, reminiscent of the Salle de Bal bosquet at the Palace of Versailles. A beloved American elm shades

OPPOSITE: The table is set for brunch in this garden oasis. A marble lazy Susan keeps pastries within reach, while collected items, such as the "For a Good Girl" mug crafted by Nantucket artist Jeanne van Etten, add charm to the tablescape. ABOVE: The faux bois pot and mugs for serving tea are a nod to the natural surroundings. The mohair throw and print-block and embroidered pillows provide comfort to the teak chairs. A pedestal urn brims with shade-loving plants, including coleus, ferns, and begonias.

the circular terrace laid in irregularly shaped stone and planted with Isotoma white star creeper to soften the edges. Surrounding the terrace is a slope lushly planted with ostrich and lady fern, Annabelle and paniculata hydrangea, and American red maple along with sweet woodruff, vinca minor, and English ivy. Pedestal urns are filled with shade-loving plants, including coleus, fern, and begonia, to add allure. This sequestered shady niche lends itself beautifully to small intimate gatherings—an evening candlelight dinner, dancing under the stars, or a weekend brunch—to celebrate the perfect summer morning on Nantucket. With its sophisticated and casual style, Nantucket Looms creates intimate outdoor spaces for relaxing and entertaining.

3
—
Our Weaving Heritage

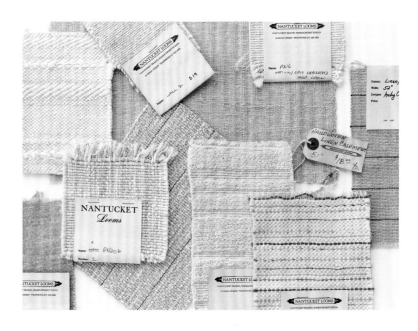

A TRADITION OF TEXTILES

On Monday, April 1, 1968, Andy Oates and Bill Euler opened Nantucket Looms, a production weaving studio and retail shop that showcased the work of talented local artists. Andy, a master weaver, managed the design and production of hand-loomed fabrics that became a major industry on the island. Bill was the shop's operations manager. Together, they cultivated lasting relationships with craftspeople and artists, whose work became important elements of their evolving Nantucket cottage style. Both possessed a keen eye for design as well as an ability to recognize talent. Marked by an atmosphere of congeniality, friendliness, and good humor, Nantucket Looms became the heart of the island where everyone was welcome.

Bill had been schooled in the art of hospitality as manager of The Plaza, the famous hotel in New York City. Andy followed a different path. After completing his degree at the Rhode Island School of Design, Andy studied photography and weaving with Anni and Josef Albers at Black Mountain College, located in the mountains of North Carolina. Black Mountain College is regarded as one of the most influential modernist art schools of the twentieth century where the unique relationship between American

Arts and Crafts style and the fine arts was emphasized. And it was at Black Mountain College where Andy first embraced the open and creative spirit of the Bauhaus, as exemplified by his eager willingness to experiment and try new techniques and ways of doing things. "Andy was a son of the Bauhaus, and I am a grandson," said Sam Kasten, former Nantucket Looms weaver and Andy's mentee. The Bauhaus was an art school founded in Weimar, Germany, in 1919 that united the disciplines of art, craft, and technology with an emphasis on functional modern design.

At Nantucket Looms, craftsmanship was, and still is, an art form that transcends style and time. As a master weaver, Andy prized texture and color. Sam said Andy considered it high praise when his work was described as "nothing," a description that emphasized the simplicity and luxurious understatement in his designs. One of Andy's fabrics was selected by Gaston Berthelot, a Christian Dior designer based in New York City. Berthelot chose "a soft white wool interwoven with narrow strips of velvet and satin ribbon in different shades of green and yellow," wrote Marianne Herlitz for *The Inquirer and Mirror* in Nantucket on March 7, 1968. "It is a luxurious fabric that can only be made on a hand loom."

PAGES 210–211: A cache of spools of cotton fibers organized by color in the Nantucket Looms weaving studio. **PAGE 212:** In preparation for weaving, bobbins are wound with different fibers, including cotton, silk, and chenille. **PAGE 213:** A monochromatic array of woven upholstery samples.
ABOVE: Seated at the loom is Sam Kasten, who began his weaving career as an apprentice to Andy Oates in the 1970s.

Andy designed prolifically for the architectural firm, Skidmore, Owings & Merrill. For a new hotel in South Africa, he used a yarn called ramie, an eco-friendly fiber used in ancient Egypt. Andy sourced yarn mostly from New Zealand and, in the spirit of the Bauhaus, designed patterns that were hand woven into upholstery fabrics, curtains, bed coverlets, and dusters. "I gave him ideas of the kind of patterns I liked and then he would adapt the design," Grace Grossman, a Nantucket Looms benefactor, was quoted as saying in February 1970. Andy wove both restoration and contemporary fabrics, and at one

time he was the only weaver in the United States to make the warp-printed fabrics prized for their luscious soft tapestry-like feeling.

In the weaving studio there were a variety of looms: a 10-foot loom that was used for weaving rugs, a 56-inch loom for making fabrics, and 40-inch looms for creating narrower widths of fabric and apparel, such as scarves and wraps. Andy worked at a loom in the middle of the shop where he and Bill employed, in the early days, nine island women who helped with the weaving and some of the selling. Bill "refused to label the merchandise with price tags," his assistant Liz Winship remembered. Instead, Liz said, "Bill preferred that the floor staff initiate friendly conversation with the customers," which was "fine," she added with a smile, "until the shop became crowded with people."

The retail shop was furnished with an eclectic mix of merchandise unique to Nantucket: bolts of handwoven cottons, linens, silks, and woolens, hand-crocheted mohair Afghans, woven candy-colored blankets and rugs. And in a showcase, there were scrimshaw and whalebone pieces, needlepoint and crewel pin cushions, ivory acorn-shaped thimble holders, delicate love beads, every size and shape of Nantucket lightship baskets, and always plants. Today it is illegal to carve whalebone or sell it in the US, unless it was sourced before 1973. "People visited the shop a few times a week with things to sell and now and then someone would come in with something beautiful," Liz said. "Andy and Bill would always take the time to look at someone's work of art or craft."

Nantucket Looms became a magnet for revered style influencers. "Private jets flew in, the passengers came to the Looms, and then the jets flew out," Sam said. "The Looms was really unusual." It was the architecture, the textiles, the tweeds, and the one-of-a-kind chief petty officer (CPO) jacket that was unique to Nantucket Looms. The CPO style was hand sewn by island tailor Lia Marks with the Nantucket Looms handwoven fabric, lined with a Liberty of London print, and finished with whalebone or ivory buttons. Actor Dustin Hoffman was fitted for one in the shop, and so was Tom Selleck, Liz remembered. Fred Rogers, the beloved host of *Mr. Roger's Neighborhood* and a Nantucket resident, filmed one of his earlier episodes at Nantucket Looms, bringing his television audience into the weaving studio for a lesson on weaving. The closing scene of the episode

ABOVE TOP: Andy weaving on a Macomber loom in the late 1970s.
ABOVE AND RIGHT: Bespoke details of CPO (chief petty officer) jackets tailored by Lia Marks in the 1970s for Nantucket Looms. The handwoven tweed is lined with a Liberty of London fabric.

ABOVE: Fashion designer Bill Blass, who was good friends with Andy and Bill, is shown wearing a Nantucket Looms boatneck sweater in the late 1970s. He often visited Nantucket Looms where he found inspiration for his collections. BELOW: A canopy bed in the primary bedroom suite at Bunny Mellon's former house on Nantucket is layered with a 'Sconset rose-hued blanket handwoven at Nantucket Looms. Bunny often appointed her homes with artfully folded handwoven throws as can be seen on the painted miniature blanket chest placed at the foot of the bed.

featured a smiling Mr. Rogers standing in the shop's doorway sporting a handwoven scarf in the classic twill weave pattern that is still in use today. Bill and Andy designed the first cotton sweater, a boatneck style with saddle-stitch shoulders and bracelet-length sleeves, to be worn by itself. They gifted one to their friend, fashion designer Bill Blass, who also took home a pair of rustic twig Adirondack chairs. Andy and Bill also sourced yardage from used nuns' habits to create challis whaler-styled shirts that were finished with whalebone buttons.

One day in the late 1960s, a number of people that appeared to be friends popped into the shop to browse, laughing and clearly having a good time, according to Sam. In the group were former First Lady Jacqueline Kennedy Onassis, American horticulturist, art collector, and philanthropist Bunny Mellon, French fashion designer Hubert de Givenchy, interior decorator Billy Baldwin, and the former actress Grace Kelly who was by then Princess Grace of Monaco, the latter garbed in a Nantucket sweatshirt paired with her trademark turban and cat-eyed sunglasses.

Bunny Mellon, who had a house on the island, was often at the shop, according to Liz. "She had a special appreciation for objects made by hand," Sam said, "and believed the slightly different colors produced by different dye lots was part of the beauty of the object." Dressed in her ubiquitous denim skirt, blue or white top, little floppy hat, and sometimes a string of pearls, Bunny propped herself up on a stool behind the counter and did what she loved to do—blend in. Since she appeared to be a staff member, "customers asked for her help with a sweater, or whatever they needed help with," Liz said, "and had no idea who she was, which was of supreme delight to her." Bunny and Andy were close friends who collaborated on various projects and kept up a lively correspondence for many years, sharing thoughts about houses and gardens and ideas and plans for projects. Frequently each one openly expressed a deep appreciation for their friendship. In one of Bunny's letters to Andy she wrote, "I told Jackie I feel you really are a true friend to me."

I. M. Pei "spent a lot of money at Nantucket Looms," Sam said. Pei was the architect of the East Building of the National Gallery of Art of which Bunny Mellon's husband, Paul Mellon, was a trustee. Pei commissioned Andy to cover the walls of the Gallery's executive boardroom with his linen and ramie heavy rib fabric. Sam

ABOVE: From the 1960s Nantucket Looms archives is this mohair throw, handwoven in various hues of brown. RIGHT: This brightly colored shirt was tailored from a silk fabric created by D.D. and Leslie Tillett, designers and owners of the Cloth Company from 1965 to 1968. The silk scarf was screen-printed by the Cloth Company. Lia Marks made the eyeglass case from handwoven overshot at Nantucket Looms in the 1970s.

said, "We wove thousands of yards in ten-inch widths, which was railroaded for upholstered walls in many of America's top corporate boardrooms, foyers, and executive spaces, as well as museums." Even Billy Baldwin used this fabric on his Knoll and Dunbar furniture lines. Thirty-five years later Sam received a phone call from the National Gallery of Art. "Are you still making that linen ramie?" the caller asked. "While it looks perfect in the boardroom—the doors that had been wrapped in the fabric are now deteriorating. Everyone was always touching the fabric as they passed through the doorways and soiling the fabric, and the gallery hoped to freshen the doors. The essence of the fabric and of Andy's design was perfect when it was chosen, and it was perfect thirty years later," Sam said. And when asked what was so beautiful about Andy's linen ramie, he added, "Nothing. And that's what's beautiful about it. There isn't a pattern."

"Dear Sir," Jacqueline Kennedy Onassis wrote in a letter to Nantucket Looms, "The whale skin bracelet that you so touchingly gave to me for John (her son) today, has had such an effect on all the little cousins here tonight—they all want one for Christmas—but only for the boys—to the chagrin of the girls. Could you possibly do me the great favor of wrapping and sending them all over the globe for Christmas? And could you be kind enough to put a little card in each that describes it as a whale skin bracelet as that is the magical thing to them. If whaling is your mythology, if you grow up looking out towards Nantucket. Each blue envelope contains the cards for each family. Please put my blue card and your description card inside each little box. And on the outside of the mailing wrapping—could you please write on the upper corner FROM Onassis. That way, in the rush at Christmas, we know which are the presents from our family. It made Anne and me so happy to see you today. Thank you for everything."

Jackie snacked while shopping at Nantucket Looms. In lieu of the "Please do not bring ice cream into the store"

ABOVE: The renowned interior designer Billy Baldwin's red slipper chair is draped with an ochre-hued mohair throw at Andy and Bill's Bear Street house. This chair, a Baldwin signature piece, is upholstered in a Nantucket Looms handwoven custom-dyed linen and cotton yarn called Nantucket Red. **LEFT:** Baldwin used this linen and ramie heavy rib fabric that Andy created for his Knoll and Dunbar furniture lines. **RIGHT:** The Nantucket home Baldwin decorated for writer Michael Gardine and his partner, Way Bandy, the famous makeup artist, as seen in 1980. The living room was an elegant, minimalist environment. The handwoven rug beneath a grouping of slipper chairs, bowls used as ashtrays, a collection of shells, and potted plants added to the serenity. The chairs were upholstered in another one of Baldwin's favorite Nantucket Looms fabrics—a handwoven mop cotton.

sign posted by the front door, Jackie often shopped with an ice cream cone in one hand, which "melted everywhere!" Liz exclaimed. Jackie also stopped at the market next door for cherries in season. On another shopping trip Jackie brought her young son, John Jr., along with her, and while she shopped, one of the weavers took the little boy upstairs to a sewing machine, held him on her lap and helped him sew a potholder for his mother. A very happy Jackie left the shop that day clasping the hand of her young son with one hand and with a very special potholder in the other.

Despite efforts to maintain secrecy, in the spring of 1980 Jackie drew attention when she accompanied Andy and Sam to Lord & Taylor's "preview before the preview," an opening party to celebrate the arts and crafts of Nantucket in "Focus America: Nantucket," a sixteen-day-long show. "Weavers weaving, woodcarvers carving, basketmakers at work," reported Anne-Marie Schiro on April 10, 1980 in the *New York Times*. "Not what you'd expect to see in a Fifth Avenue department store. But

those are some of the sights that will greet shoppers at Lord & Taylor this month, for the store is celebrating Nantucket and the island's crafts heritage." According to store vice president and frequent island visitor Peggy Kaufman, "Lord & Taylor was first drawn to Nantucket because of the Islanders' very special interpretation of typically American arts and crafts that can be traced back to the days when it was the greatest whaling center in the world." The entire length of the fifth floor was converted into small shops representing Nantucket's Main Street and filled with loom-woven throws, antiques, handcrafted furniture, handwoven baskets, wood and ivory carvings, prints and etchings, and pine carvings of birds. An additional five rooms open to the public were designed to reflect what Peggy described as Nantucket's "classic American approach to fashion and design." Sam rounded out the exhibition with his weaving demonstration on a loom transported from Nantucket Looms.

Jackie commissioned Andy to weave the fabrics for her Martha's Vineyard house designed by Hugh Newell

Jacobsen, and she enjoyed collecting decoupage boxes handcrafted by Leslie Linsley for Nantucket Looms. Hubert de Givenchy thought the macramé belts on display were what he described as "sauvage" and used them in one of his collections. Billy Baldwin, probably the "most elegant human being that ever walked the earth," Sam said, "was a consummate gentleman." The "Great American Decorator," who beautified the houses of Truman Capote's swans, the nickname Capote used to describe his close friends that included Babe Paley and Lee Radziwill, Jackie's sister, who especially loved the modern handsewn quilts at Nantucket Looms. Baldwin lived on Nantucket for the last ten years of his life and was great friends with Andy and Bill and visited the shop almost every day.

The Shop: Textiles and Furnishings

In December 1966, the Cloth Company of Nantucket announced in the local newspaper, *The Inquirer and Mirror*, that they planned to open a general gift and Christmas shop. Islanders were invited to craft ornaments, gifts, toys, and games in fabric, wood, clay, or other materials. This was the beginning of the retail shop that was renamed Nantucket Looms, which opened on April 1, 1968, at 16 Main Street under the new ownership of Andy and Bill. While the shop offerings were limited and somewhat varied, it was the start of what would become the top retail destination on the island.

In the summer of 1974, Liz was asked to come help out in the shop for two weeks—and stayed for forty years. "A day at Nantucket Looms was like being at an eight-hour cocktail party with no drinks," Stephanie Hall, Liz's former assistant, remembered. "Like a great bartender, Liz knew everyone's name and made everyone feel special." Maria Mitchell, a Nantucket astronomer who in 1847 discovered a comet that later became known as "Miss Mitchell's Comet," had this to say about the daring daughters of Nantucket: "The woman who does her work better than ever women did before, helps all womankind, not only now, but in all the future—she moves the whole race no matter if it is only a differential movement—it is growth." This applies equally to Liz Winship. Liz is a great teacher, and her personality is magnetic. People came to the shop just to see her. Aside from her joyous and effervescent spirit, there's a really good reason for that. Like her customer Bunny Mellon, who "worked" with her behind the counter on occasion, Liz has what former First

OPPOSITE: The Nantucket Looms staff congregates in front of the shop at 16 Main Street in 1976. Back row, from left: Lillian Foster, Dorothy Backus, Sam Kasten, Ani Kasten, Jane Kasten, Bill Euler, Liz Winship. Center, from left: Deborah Hatch, Mary Malden, Andy Oates, Anna Worth, Jamie Gould. Front row, from left: Laura Lovett, Linda Ballinger. **ABOVE**: In 2001, Liz calls attention to the lined handwoven CPO jacket, a popular Nantucket Looms product.

Lady "Lady Bird" Johnson, who was also a Nantucket Looms customer, described as a "working at it kind of knowledge." Sometimes the results of Liz's work were immediate, as in the case of a client searching for the perfect Nantucket color to paint on the interior walls of her house. "Fog," Liz suggested, the color of the Gray Lady's atmosphere, and "fog" was used to high acclaim. Then, there were the other times when one had to wait—sometimes years—for the magic to happen. As in the case of Arie Kopelman, the former president of Chanel. Arie commented that his objective was always to "delight and surprise" Chanel's customers. When on Nantucket, Arie often visited Nantucket Looms to "see what's new." On one of his walks downtown, a birds-eye maple secretary displayed in the shop's large window caught his eye. "That piece drove me crazy," he said, "but Liz wouldn't sell it." He said he spent the next ten years "drooling." He had to have it. Year after year Arie asked Liz if he could buy the secretary, and every year she refused, telling him it was a "permanent part of the window display." Finally, she agreed to sell it to him. Arie said, "Nantucket Looms is my kind of shop. There's a feeling about it. Whether it's a woven piece or whatever. It's where I walk in to see what's new and say, 'I love this.' Could be a wicker étagère or anything. I found four pillows at the Looms. I'd looked everywhere, and there they were. And I love how they merchandise things."

It was Liz's boundless energy that kept the shop looking fresh and different every day. By rearranging furnishings, setting up new displays, and styling vignettes, she provided opportunities for her clientele to visualize merchandise in their own homes. Liz's gift of sharing stories about the artists' and weavers' techniques, as well as the history behind the antique pieces and local crafts, created a connection to the island. Liz championed the next generation of artists and artisans by nurturing their creativity and providing input and feedback into what she knew would sell. For example, she suggested alternative color palettes, types of model boats, or different shorebird carvings. Liz encouraged them to push their boundaries so they would be successful.

The Interior Design Studio

In the mid-1990s Liz gradually began to take on small design requests from shop customers, one by one bringing Nantucket Looms cottage-style sensibility to homes on Nantucket and elsewhere. "It was the natural thing to do," she said. Customers became clients by simply asking her to visit their homes to "have a look." New York City playwright Judy Seinfeld was captivated by Liz's "lightness of being" and commented that her extraordinary "ability to arrange things draws you

RIGHT: Weavers at work on looms set up for weaving throws in the Nantucket Looms studio today. The spools on the shelves are displayed in a rainbow of colors. The Nantucket Looms compass rose billboard, originally attached to the side of the building at 16 Main Street, hangs on the wall. PAGE 225: In preparation for the weaving process, yarn is wound on bobbins with a bobbin winder.

right in." Decorating Judy's house was a team effort. "We just kept moving things around until we were pleased with the effect," Judy said. By 1998 Nantucket Looms had established a full-scale interior design business.

An advocate for the pay-it-forward philosophy, Liz, upon her retirement, bequeathed the business to three women who carry on Nantucket's formidable legacy of producing strong, spirited, and independent women. Liz's daughter, Bess Clarke, grew up on Nantucket. "I guess you could say I've been there all along," Bess said, "including the Christmas photo of the staff in 1976 when Liz was pregnant with me." Now Nantucket Looms CEO, Bess said, "I wasn't ever allowed to touch the cash drawer when I was a kid, and I was so intimidated by Bill Euler. And now, I manage the finances and have his old set of keys and wallet in my drawer." Bess serves on various nonprofit boards benefiting the Nantucket community. She shared, "I love the business management of Nantucket Looms and interacting with the customers. I know everything 'under the hood' of the business, but prefer to leave the creative process to the team." It would not be surprising to see her sweeping the sidewalks along Main Street. "It's Liz's work ethic that I modeled," Bess said. "Don't ask someone to do it unless you are prepared to do it yourself. I am grateful for this life we've created. It's so wonderful how it all has worked out."

THE ART OF WEAVING

Nowhere is the romance of weaving more evident than in the studio hidden above Nantucket Looms Main Street retail shop. "It's the best kept secret on Nantucket," Bess said. This is where the magic is, where the creation of soft and sumptuous handwovens happens every weekday. The peaceful sights and sounds of the floor looms at work, combined with the luxurious feel of natural fibers, awaken one's sense of touch and desire for the finest.

Master Weaver Rebecca Jusko Peraner began working at Nantucket Looms as an intern sorting catalog fabric samples. A graduate of Rhode Island School of Design, she arrived on Nantucket shortly after graduation in 1995 choosing to make it her home. "When they put me on a mohair throw warp, that was it," Rebecca said. "I knew what I wanted to do." Two all knowledgeable and wonderful weavers, Linda Ballinger, Andy Oates's niece, and Karin Sheppard, Lia Mark's daughter, mentored Rebecca in the traditions of Nantucket Looms weaving, and in "absorbing the dynamics of life on Nantucket," Rebecca said. Apprenticing with Andy taught Rebecca the time-tested techniques of creating one-of-a-kind textiles and how to look at everything in a creative way "knowing a little bit of your soul is woven into this thing you've made," Rebecca said. Practice makes perfect, and mistakes are welcome. In handwovens today there is a nuance of the hand and touch. The imperfections are the beauty. Imperfect perfection is the desired result.

It's always a lovely surprise for Rebecca when she sees someone wearing or using a handwoven she made. Her favorite occasion is when she notices a baby blanket that's turned into a child's lovie and kept under their pillow. Rebecca reminisces about the time soon after she began weaving at Nantucket Looms when she and her mother were dining at American Seasons on Centre Street, and she spotted a woman wearing a yellow-and-white mohair wrap in a tabby weave, simple and elegant. "I think I made that," she told her mother. "That feeling, accompanied by the burst of pride on my mother's face, brought warm feelings of fulfillment, pride, humbleness—the whole gamut," she said. "It was pretty special."

Today, as a co-owner of Nantucket Looms and director of the weaving studio, Rebecca and her team craft high-quality handwoven textiles, blankets and throws, scarves and wraps, and table linens using time-honored techniques and patterns. Only fine natural fibers are used—linen, mohair, ramie, cotton, cashmere, and wool—in a palette inspired by the hues of the island and surrounding sea.

Five Macomber looms dominate the light-filled production weaving studio above the retail space at 51 Main Street, a brick building that was rebuilt after the Great Fire of 1846. Throughout the day rhythmic sounds from the looms' keyboards of pedals are complemented by the thump of beaters pressing weft against warp. The studio has a vaulted ceiling with layers of deep crown molding.

ABOVE: An array of yarn is threaded through a tension box as the warps are wound. BELOW: A basket filled with spools of cotton yarn. OPPOSITE: An assemblage of tools used during the weaving process that includes a tension box, a shuttle wrapped with yarn, a pair of shears for cutting, a weaving hook and needle, tubes of yarn and a rug shuttle, a crank that is part of the loom, a mohair yarn brush, and label tape used to finish every textile.

Three large northwest-facing windows open the space to a great and welcoming natural light. An abundance of handwoven scarves, throws, wraps, blankets, and table linens draped from railings and stacked in tasteful displays tantalize the lucky visitor who finds their way up the backstairs to the hidden studio. One wall is filled with spools of natural fibers and yarns wound onto cones and sorted by color. In a nearby corner stands a latched-door cupboard washed in a coat of blue paint that appears as old as the building. Stacked on the shelves inside are links to Nantucket Looms's past—a collection of fabric swatches—or samples—handwoven throughout the decades. Each sample tells the story of a time and place and illustrates a weaving method or technique.

Rebecca speaks to the traditions of the Nantucket Looms weaving style, one of which former customer Hubert de Givenchy heartily adhered to in his own atelier in Paris. And that is to let the characteristics of the yarns speak for themselves. Nowhere is this more evident than in the fabric Rebecca wove, a pattern of her own design, for another French company—Chanel. Working with the designers at Peter Marino's International office, she sampled several variations of a textural dense fabric not knowing what the finished application would be. Rebecca said that "as a textile designer you try to create interesting textures and variations with the yarn as your brush. Having a wide range of all natural fibers, weights, and colors is like a painter's palette." What she found so intriguing about the Chanel project was "the juxtaposition of the full bouncy wool bouclé yarn and the flat stark natural linen warp that encompass the wool and the darker navy/black color, making certain attributes of the fabric float between a foreground and background." The Chanel invoice reads, "black/cream fabric, heavy warp with cloudy cream weft." The 54-inch–wide upholstery fabric, woven with wool, linen, and cotton, was used in Chanel's showrooms in Hong Kong, Korea, and Taiwan. This is precisely the exquisite dynamic, the simple construct found in all Nantucket Looms handwoven designs that allows the yarn to speak for itself.

In the 1990s Rebecca worked with a designer on the interior fabrics for an early Melinda and Bill Gates private jet. For this project she wove a silk herringbone for the interior walls and an "irregular twill" weave of linen in blues and grays along with cotton canvas for the backs of the seats to complement the leather seat cushions.

Other unique fabric orders have been designed for Ronay Arit and Richard Menschel of New York City, as well as award-winning architect Hugh Newel Jacobsen, interior designers Michael S. Smith and Naomi Leff, American businessman Herb Siegel, and many more. Richard Menschel said, "Nantucket Looms has great taste and design instincts." The Menschels also collected Mark Sutherland's scale-model boats, Pat Gardner's painted and carved birds, and colorful raku balls, a type of Japanese pottery they display in their homes and give as wedding gifts—all from Nantucket Looms. Many of Rebecca's handwoven textiles have found their way into places where people live—be it an apartment, a house or mansion, an office, a plane, or boat. Some customers when traveling pack a throw or blanket in their suitcases to bring a bit of home along for the trip. According to Rebecca, "Whether they're year-round people, summer residents, or visitors from around the world, Looms customers have adorned their houses with Nantucket

Looms magic and gifted Looms handwoven textiles for all sorts of occasions." Rebecca said she particularly enjoys working hand in hand with the Nantucket Looms Interior Design Studio to design distinctive patterns and create extra special handwovens for the finished touch.

Nantucket Looms Today

Nantucket Looms is located at 51 Main Street in a two-story brick mid-nineteenth-century era building, shaded by a canopy of trees, and just a short walk up the cobblestoned street from the harbor within earshot of the peeling of the church bells at the Second Congregational Meeting House Society. Since that memorable day in 1968 when Andrew Oates and William Euler opened the doors of Nantucket Looms at 16 Main Street for the first time, and the years of Liz Winship's charismatic leadership that followed—what was true then is still true today. Showcasing the work of local craftspeople and artists remains

LEFT: Holding a shuttle wound with a weft yarn in her hand, a weaver passes it back and forth across the warp during the weaving process. The projecting horizontal wooden piece of the loom in front of her arm is called the beater because it is used to beat the weft yarn against the warp yarn. In the background, throws and blankets are displayed against the weaving studio wall. **ABOVE:** A weaver winding a warp—threading yarn through the tension box. A warp is the set of vertical threads in a woven textile. An array of finished throws is seen in the background.

at the heart of the business with works gracing countless homes on Nantucket, and around the world. Taking pride in the luxurious handwovens created in the second-floor weaving studio, the next generations of owners know it's important that there's always something new to see in the shop. The interior design studio's work, featured within the pages of this book, continues to evolve while staying true to the vision that the business was founded upon. The partnership that connects Bess Clarke, Stephanie Hall, and Rebecca Jusko Peraner is one rooted in honoring the traditions of Nantucket Looms and carrying its legacy forward. The gratitude to Andy Oates, Bill Euler, and Liz Winship is always present for passing down not only their industry knowledge but for modeling a consistent life of purpose while maintaining a spirit of generosity.

NANTUCKET LOOMS HANDWOVEN TEXTILES

**LINEN CRACKLE BLOCK WEAVE
IN CELADON**

**COTTON AND LINEN RIBBED
WEAVE IN ECRU**

**MOHAIR TWILL WEAVE IN IVORY
WITH SILK ACCENTS**

**ALPACA TWILL WEAVE IN A 2-INCH
STRIPE IN SHADES OF BLUE**

THESE PAGES AND FOLLOWING PAGES: An array of textiles from over fifty years of weaving.
OPPOSITE: An alpaca throw in a twill weave with hand-knotted fringe in spring green.

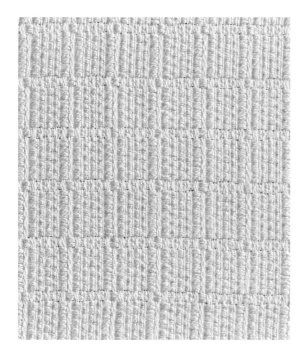

LINEN AND SILK OVERSHOT
COLUMN WEAVE IN IVORY

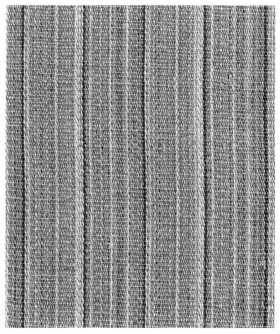

LINEN TABBY STRIPE WEAVE IN SHADES
OF GREEN, GRAY, AND PURPLE

COTTON AND LINEN TABBY WEAVE
IN BLUES AND CREAMS

SILK CRACKLE STRIPE
WEAVE IN GRAY

OPPOSITE: A cashmere throw in a herringbone weave in variegated
shades of blues, greens, and grays with hand-knotted tufted fringe.

Acknowledgments

O n behalf of the Nantucket Looms family, we would like to thank our "mother"— Liz Winship, who has inspired us with her work ethic and generous spirit; the team at Rizzoli: Publisher Charles Miers and our editor Sandy Gilbert Freidus; and our talented graphic designer, David Byars; Linda Jane Holden for her willingness to understand every aspect of our story; and Matt Kisiday for his patience and exacting eye. To our skilled weavers and shop staff, and to our committed design team: Tracey Goncalves, Brooke Gherardini, and Amy Tejada. To Lindsay Freter, who was a part of this process every step of the way; and to Thayer Hale and Claire McElwain for their behind-the-scenes support. To the Nantucket Historical Association and Bobby Frazier for their invaluable archives. We extend our heartfelt thanks to the homeowners who graciously opened their homes to us: Lauren and Chris Casazza, Mary and Matt Claus, Emmy and Charlie Kilvert, Tom Kim and John Olsen, Holly and Mark Maisto, Suzy and Gary McCarthy, Ann and Craig Muhlhauser, Christine, Edward, Henry, and Amy Sanford, and Liz and Todd Winship. To our families for their love. To Jim and Mary Bennett, Corinne Nevinny, and Wendy Schmidt for their understanding of the importance of preserving what is special to Nantucket. And finally, to our clients and customers who are the reason we open our doors every morning.

—BESS CLARKE, STEPHANIE HALL, REBECCA JUSKO PERANER

W ith deepest appreciation and lasting gratitude to the Rizzoli team: Publisher Charles Miers; and to my amazing and extraordinary editor Sandy Gilbert Freidus. To our remarkable book designer, David Byars, and to copy editor Meg Downey, whose superior command of the English language was invaluable. To Nantucket Looms matriarch and wonderful friends, Liz and Todd Winship. To Nantucket Looms partners: Bess Clarke, Stephanie Hall, and Rebecca Jusko Peraner, who provided invaluable guidance and insight to me about the Nantucket Looms brand. And to the talented Nantucket Looms artists and artisans featured in this book: Joan Albaugh, Hillary Anapol, Susan and Michael Bacle, Susan Boardman, Barbara Clarke, M.J. Levy Dickson, Julie Gifford, Kenneth Layman, Julija Mostykanova, Rebecca Jusko Peraner, Mark Sutherland, Jocelyn Sandor Urban, and David Wiggins. And thanks go to Linda Darby Ballinger, Mary Randolph Ballinger, Laura Cooper Davison, Charlie Gerow, Peggi Godwin, Jamie Gould, Michael Harrison, Debbie Hatch, LeRoy Henderson, David Holden, Julie Jordin, Sam Kasten, Arie L. Kopelman, Richard Menschel, Craig Muhlhauser, Brooke Shealy Myatt, Jennifer Nieling, Katie Rainier, Judy Seinfeld, Karin Sheppard, and Steve Tees—all of whom shed light on many aspects of the rich history of Nantucket Looms on an island thirty miles out to sea.

—LINDA JANE HOLDEN

Notes & Credits

Unless otherwise stated, all quotations were obtained by writer Linda Jane Holden from interviews or correspondence.

Interviews were conducted by Linda Jane Holden with the following people:

Nantucket Looms artists and artisans: Joan Albaugh, Hillary Anapol, Susan and Michael Bacle, Susan Boardman, Barbara Clarke, M.J. Levy Dickson, Julie Gifford, Kenneth Layman, Julija Mostykanova, Rebecca Jusko Peraner, Mark Sutherland, Jocelyn Sandor Urban, David Wiggins, September 2023-June 2024. Profiles were written about Lia Marks, based on documents and interviews with Lia's daughter Karin Sheppard, August 2023; and Mark McNair, based on documents and interviews with Liz Winship, August 2023, and Michael Bacle, March 2024.

Nantucket Looms past and current employees: Linda Darby Ballinger, former weaver and Andy Oates's niece, August 2023; Bess Clarke, CEO and partner, May 2023-May 2024; Jamie Gould, former weaver and owner and president, Rogers and Goffigan Ltd., June 2024; Stephanie Hall, principal designer and partner, August 2023-January 2024; Debbie Hatch, former staff member, September 2023-June 2024; Sam Kasten, former weaver, June-July 2023; Rebecca Jusko Peraner, master weaver and partner, May 2023-June 2024; Karin Shepard, former weaver, August 2023; Liz Winship, partner, August 2023-May 2024.

Nantucket homeowners who asked to remain anonymous: August 2023-March 2024.

Additional interviews: Laura Cooper Davison, garden manager and designer, Sean O'Callaghan Landscaping, August 2023-March 2024; Michael Harrison, chief curator and Obed Macy research chair, Nantucket Historical Association, August 2023; Arie L. Kopelman, former president, Chanel, August 2023; Richard Menschel, investment banker, February 2024; Phyllis Ross, author, The Fabric of Activism: The Design Works of Bedford Stuyvesant, (New York: Fordham University Press), to be published in 2025, March-June 2024; Judy Seinfield, artist, August 2023; Barbara Beinecke Spitler, daughter of Walter Beinecke Jr., August 2023; Seth Tillett, son of D.D. and Leslie Tillett, March 2024.

OTHER SOURCES:

Page 29: "old almost forgotten techniques of weaving," Letter from Jacqueline Kennedy Onassis to Letitia Baldrige, May 19, 1970, Subject Files: Bedford Stuyvesant, John F. Kennedy Presidential Library and Museum.

Page 38: "Nantucket! Take out your map . . ." Herman Melville, *Moby Dick* (New York: W. W. Norton & Company, Inc., 1851, 1976 edition), 62.

Page 38: "the wondrous traditional story . . ." Melville, *Moby Dick*, 63.

Page 43: "pieces of wood in Nantucket . . ." Melville, *Moby Dick*, 62.

Pages 48–49: "If you had a lot of money, . . ." Andy Oates, oral history interview by Nancy Newhouse, October 13, 1999, MS495-32, 1999, Nantucket Historical Association Archives.

Page 56: "that's a big deal . . ." Larry Lindner, "Julija Mostykanova Feeney's Unlikely Journey to the Top of the Art Scene," *Nantucket Current*, June 24, 2022, n-magazine.com.

Page 84: "opportunity to recognize that we have problems . . ." Noelle Barton, "Nantucket Designated as 'Endangered Place,'" *Cape Cod Times*, June 27, 2000, capecodtimes.com.

Page 84: "These new people don't share bathrooms. . . ." Tom Congdon, "Nantucket Nouveau," *Forbes*, September 6, 1999, forbes.com.

Page 88: "My houses are expensive to build, . . ." Joseph Giovannini, "Hugh Newell Jacobsen Crafts a Modernist Haven in Maine," *Architectural Digest*, May 2009, architecturaldigest.com.

Page 90: "You are always taking books off the shelves . . ." Erik Heywood, "Architect Hugh Newell Jacobsen and His Egg-Crate Bookshelves," *Forbes*, July 28, 2010, forbes.com.

Page 90: "good architecture never shouts. . . ." Kathy Orton, "Hugh Newell Jacobsen, Award-winning Modernist Architect Dies at 91," *Washington Post*, March 4, 2021.

Page 125: "hearing the whistle of wigs . . ." Noah Davis, "The Hand of the Master," *Modern Huntsman*, Volume 11, September 2023, 101–105.

Page 205: "the quintessential Nantucket boat, after the whale boat . . ." Michael Harrison, "The Origins of the Rainbow Fleet," *Historic Nantucket*, Fall 2018, 34–35.

Pages 213–214: "a soft white wool interwoven with narrow strips of velvet and satin ribbon . . ." Marianne Herlitz, "Interview Portraits," *The Inquirer and Mirror*, March 7, 1968, Nantucket Looms Archive.

Page 214: "I gave him ideas of the kind of patterns I liked and then he would adapt the design . . ." Virginia Bohlin (interview with Mrs. Grace Grossman, a Nantucket Looms' benefactor), "One Woman's Hobby Saves an Industry," *The Herald Traveler*, February 15, 1970, 16–17.

Pages 216–217: "You must know . . ." Correspondence between Andrew Oates and Bunny Mellon, 1981–1984, private archive.

Pages 217: "Dear Sir . . ." Jacqueline Kennedy Onassis letter to Nantucket Looms, Nantucket Looms Archive.

Page 220: "Weavers weaving, woodcarvers carving . . ." Anne-Marie Schiro, "For Nantucket Craftsmen, Fifth Avenue Debut," *New York Times*, April 10, 1980.

Page 220: "Lord & Taylor was first drawn to Nantucket . . ." Peggy Kaufman, Lord & Taylor press release, 1980, Nantucket Looms Archive.

Page 221: "The woman who does her work better than ever women did before . . ." Jascin N. Leonardo Finger, *The Daring Daughters of Nantucket Island: How Island Women from the Seventeenth Through the Nineteenth Centuries Lived a Life Contrary to Other American Women* (Nantucket, Massachusetts: Jack's Shack Press, 2014), 8.

Page 221: "working at it kind of knowledge." Lady Bird Johnson, *A White House Diary*, (New York: Holt, Rinehart and Winston), 1970, Nantucket Looms Archive.

PHOTOGRAPHY

All images are from the Nantucket Looms Archive unless specified otherwise below.

MATT KISIDAY: Front and back covers, endpapers, pages 4–5, 8–9, 10, 15, 18–19, 30–31, 34–35, 38–39, 43, 50–123, 125, 130–187, 198–213, 215 (bottom right), 217, 218 (bottom), 222–233, 236–237, 239. **ERIN McGINN:** Pages 2–3, 6–7, 16 (left, styled by Abby Capalbo), 26–27, 36–37 (styled by Abby Capalbo), 40–42, 44–45, 124, 128–129, 188–197, 235. **LINDSAY FRETER:** Pages 12–13, 32–33. **BARBARA CLARKE:** Pages 16–17, 32 (left). **CLAIRE McELWAIN:** page 215 (bottom left).

ARCHIVAL IMAGES

Page 28 : (above): Main Street, Nantucket, Massachusetts, P12151, PH165 Collection of Photographic Prints, 1968, Nantucket Historical Association.

Page 28: (bottom): Gentle Morning on The Far-Away Island, Nantucket, PC-Main-Square-43, in the Nantucket Postcard Collection (PH164), Nantucket Historical Association.

Page 29: (top left): Design Works lecture, photograph, early 1970s, Courtesy of the Tillett Family.

Page 43: Artwork by Leslie Tillett, Courtesy of the Tillett Family.

Page 46: (top left): *Architectural Digest*, Spring 1967.

Page 47: *Architectural Digest*, Spring 1967.

Page 49: Woodbox Inn, Piemags/DCM/Alamy Stock Photo.

Page 216: (top): Bill Blass, photograph by Joel Baldwin, from Toni Kosover's article "Bill Blass," *L'Officiel*, USA, Spring 1977.

Page 216: (bottom): Bunny Mellon canopy bed, photograph by Daniel Sutherland.

Pages 218–219: Ernst Beadle, *House & Garden*, February 1980, © Condé Nast.

ARTISTS

Pages 10, 85–87: Brice Marden, *12 Views for Caroline Tatyana*, 1979, © 2024 Estate of Brice Marden/Artists Rights Society (ARS), New York.

Page 58: Edward Weston, *Surf on Black Sand, Point Lobos*, 1938, © 2024 Center for Creative Photography, Arizona Board of Regents/Artists Rights Society (ARS), New York.

Page 62: Sebastião Salgado, *Southern Right Whale Tail, Valdés Peninsula, Argentina*, 2004, © Sebastião Salgado/SAIF, Paris 2024.

Pages 84–85, 86 (bottom, right): Josef Albers, *Homage to the Square*, print, 1966, © The Josef and Anni Albers Foundation/Artists Rights Society (ARS), New York, 2024.

Page 108: Joan Miró, *Le Cosmonaute*, aquatint, 1969, © Successió Miró/Artists Rights Society (ARS), New York/ADAGP, Paris 2024.

Pages 110–111, 112: Henry Moore, *Sculptural Ideas 2, Sculptural Ideas 5, Sculptural Ideas 3*, etching and aquatint on paper, 1980, © The Henry Moore Foundation, All Rights Reserved, DACS 2024/www.henry-moore.org.

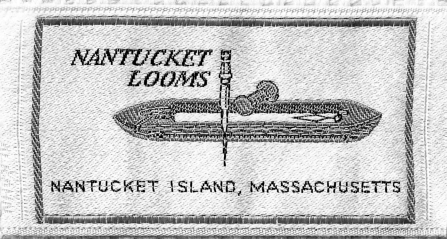

NANTUCKET ISLAND, MASSACHUSETTS

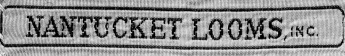

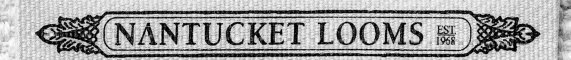

First published in the United States of America in 2025 by
Rizzoli International Publications, Inc.
49 West 27th Street
New York, NY 10001
www.rizzoliusa.com

Publisher: CHARLES MIERS
Project Editor: SANDRA GILBERT FREIDUS
Production Manager: REBECCA AMBROSE
Managing Editor: LYNN SCRABIS
Copy Editor: MEG DOWNEY
Editorial Assistance: HILARY NEY

DESIGN BY DAVID BYARS

Printed in China

2025 2026 2027 2028 / 10 9 8 7 6 5 4 3 2 1

ISBN: 978-0-8478-4658-0
Library of Congress Control Number: 2024946493

Visit us online:
Instagram.com/RizzoliBooks
Facebook.com/RizzoliNewYork
X: @Rizzoli_Books
Youtube.com/user/RizzoliNY

FRONT AND BACK ENDPAPER SPREADS: An exquisite fabric design featuring a blend of wool, linen, and cotton yarns. Created by Nantucket Looms for the House of Chanel, it was used in Chanel's Hong Kong, Korea, and Taiwan showrooms. FRONT SINGLE ENDPAPER: This striped alpaca throw, named "Buoy Blue," was handwoven in the Nantucket Looms weaving studio. BACK SINGLE ENDPAPER: This Nantucket Looms mohair throw, named "Windswept Cove," was handwoven with wool, cotton, silk, and mohair fibers. PAGES 2–3: A quaint cottage near the path to Steps Beach on Nantucket's north shore. PAGE 4: At Rantum Scooting, a Dutch door that connects the back porch to the butler's pantry is opened to allow the refreshing sea breezes to pass through. A bench provides seating while a hook rack holds all the necessities for a day at the beach. PAGES 6–7: A view of the Old North Wharf on Nantucket Harbor, where Lydia Cottage is located. PAGES 8–9: Beneath soaring blue skies, a view of Hummock Pond looking east towards Cisco Beach, a popular surfing destination. PAGE 10: Modern elements of the Nantucket Looms style are on display at the Carriage House. The sofa, draped with a cashmere throw and upholstered in fabric handwoven at Nantucket Looms, complements the prints, *12 Views for Caroline Tatyana* by Brice Marden, on the nearby wall. In the entry, the woven chair is by Gareth Neal. PAGES 12–13: Nantucket Looms understated elegance comes to this home in Osterville on Cape Cod. The soft palette of colors and modern decor are complemented by the textured stone fireplace chimney and the exposed rafters of the ceiling. PAGE 235: A bronze Victorian door knocker adds a whimsical touch to the front entryway of the Winships' home. PAGES 236–237: In the early morning light of autumn, the waves of the Atlantic Ocean break on the shoreline at Stone's Beach. PAGE 239: A collection of Nantucket Looms tags past and present (bottom) displayed on a handwoven fabric called Cotton Flake Canvas.